Dedication

This book is dedicated to the families caught in the cycle
of high conflict

Acknowledgments

Thank you to my good friend, Allyson Sammons, for your
excellent editing and bringing this into a coherent work.

Thank you to my good friend, Nichola Ranson, for your
encouragement and critical eye, once again.

D1225612

CONTENTS

INTRODUCTION

"As went the marriage so goes the divorce" and *"Stay away from the flypaper!"* These were the most important words spoken to me when I was going through my own high conflict divorce some 13 years ago. My therapist's advice changed the way I thought about nearly everything that happened from that point forward and, most importantly, how I reacted to events during the two-and-a-half year divorce process. If you have been caught up in the long and painful path of a high conflict divorce you will probably agree with these statements. If you are just beginning the divorce process, please take time to reflect on these statements. I believe they will save you great pain and help you find your way through this most treacherous time.

If you are reading this material you are likely someone who is looking (or knows someone who is looking) for answers regarding the cycle and traits of a high conflict divorce. In the pages to come I will give you a perspective that you may not hear from the established minds in the worlds of family law or mental health. My goal is to offer you a highly effective process to navigate through high conflict divorce, and get you to think outside of the traditional "box". I have developed leading-edge strategies that have been enormously successful in helping clients and students through the maze of high conflict divorce.

Most Family Court professionals believe that all parents have to find a way to co-parent and generate orders that reflect this, even in the face of clear evidence that in high conflict situations, co-parenting only makes the problem worse. These beliefs about co-parenting are based on the normal behavior of the vast majority of separated parents (around 70%). Parents in the remaining high conflict group (around 30%) are not capable of co-parenting in the traditional sense.

Familiarizing yourself with the traits and behaviors

of high conflict personalities is probably the single most important undertaking necessary to changing the way YOU think, react and behave when it comes to dealing with the other parent. It isn't advanced psychology to state that most all of our worldviews and behaviors are a product of our history.

Examining the history of your relationship, as well as any childhood issues experienced by you or the other parent, will help you not only understand better the other parent's point of view, but will give you a good predictor of the behavior to come.

This book will change how you think and what you believe regarding the family court system, and free you from the recurring nightmare of being entangled in a fight that makes no sense. It is not intended to be digested in one sitting.

"In the long run, we shape our lives, and we shape ourselves. The process never ends until we die. And the choices we make are ultimately our own responsibility."

-- Eleanor Roosevelt
(First Lady & accomplished stateswoman, 1884 - 1962)

Chapter 1

Understanding High Conflict Divorce

Time and again I encounter parents who wish they had made different choices about how much "fighting" to engage in. They say that if they had known the skills taught in our program[i], they would have done things quite differently. It is my hope that the information in this book will help you make informed choices that will alleviate the anguish of a protracted high conflict divorce.

Make no mistake about it: following in the footsteps of these other parents will be costly, if it hasn't been already. These costs are both financial and emotional. Unfortunately, the price that is paid does not stop there. Although every member of the family ends up paying in the long run, the high sensitivity of children means that they are the ones who end up feeling every disruption before, during and after the divorce the most.

You've probably heard the wonderful definition of insanity attributed to Albert Einstein: *"Insanity: doing the same thing over and over again and expecting different results."* This quote beautifully describes high conflict divorce. How do we stop the insanity? Is there another approach we can take? Yes, there is! We can make the conscious choice to take our focus off "fighting" and attend to "empowered living" instead. Such a reversal can reap untold rewards, not the least of which is the opportunity to serve as a positive role model for our children. It is an enormous gift to help them understand, by our example, what it looks like to meet the world head on, to be responsible for ourselves, and not to be dependent on anyone else.

What I am suggesting is that if, **sooner rather than later,** we focus on our children—meaning, we act as if the other parent didn't exist and there would be no help from them at all—we will find a way to make our life work and no longer worry about what is taking place when the children are with the other parent. In doing this, we will be released from the prison of the high conflict cycle and will be free to have a simpler, easier and more connected relationship with our children.

Telling someone to do something they can't or won't do is likely to cause that something to not get done. According to research in the area of high conflict divorce and custody cases, 30% of families dealing with custody issues will find themselves in a high conflict case, and as many as 60% of <u>all</u> families will be in a moderate to high conflict case[ii]. This high percentage of couples caught in the untenable situation of the high conflict group will never find their way completely out of it. Without early intervention, the remaining moderate- to high-conflict couples' time spent in conflict will be greatly protracted. Many of the high conflict parents will stay in the high conflict cycle for several years, quite possibly until their children are grown.

Here is the good news: This book offers a very different approach to dealing with high conflict divorce and custody disputes. You don't have to keep trying to do what your ex wants, or keep trying to make her/him do what you want. Walking the tightrope between these two prickly options simply does not apply here. In fact, I invite you to realize that there is another, better, healthier option. Please re-read this paragraph and then simply allow yourself to relax. **What you learn in this book and what you do as a result may be the most important part of your process of getting on with your life and disengaging from the conflict.**

Indicators of High Conflict Divorce

Here are the indicators that constitute a high conflict divorce (this includes custody fights). Take a look and see which of these indicators pertain to your case. How many of them pertain to you, personally?

- There was a large power differential in the relationship (one parent had huge control issues).

- There were extreme and frequent outbursts of anger in the relationship.

- There was a constant sense of instability in the relationship (not knowing how the other parent was going to react to a situation; a sense of bracing, or of always walking on eggshells).

- One of the parents reacts like the other parent is victimizing them.

- One of the parents complains that they feel threatened by the other parent.

- One of the parents accuses the other parent of being neglectful, damaging, absent, controlling, abusive, enmeshed or overly involved.

- Either parent alleges addiction, including prescription or street drugs, alcohol abuse, gambling, or pornography.

- Either parent accuses the other parent of being unstable, crazy, erratic, irrational, moody, or emotionally disturbed, or alleges such behavior as indicative of a personality problem or disorder.

- One of the parents complains about the safety and well-being of the children while in the other's care.

- Refusal to follow court orders.

- One parent argues that they were the primary parent before the breakup or insist that they should be the primary parent now, and refuse to agree to a parenting plan that incorporates both parent's schedules in regards to access to the children.

- One of the parents refuses to reach a child sharing agreement.

- One of the parents has filed for a restraining order alleging domestic violence, stalking, harassment, threats or physical altercations.

- One of the parents reacts in and around court hearings by displaying emotions, such as being extremely frightened, angry, hysterical, or anxious. One of the parents attacks the other with criticism.

- One of the parents seems to be deliberately provoking the other parent into reacting.

- Either parent alleges criminal behavior or possesses a criminal record.

- One of the parents accuses the other of lying.

- Child Protective Services (CPS), or any professional, has been called upon to assist the family with issues related to the welfare and/or safety of the children.

- Minor's counsel has been recommended to the case to provide a voice for the children.

- The parents argue over child sharing percentages that do not appear to be based upon valid concerns. One parent complains that the other parent has not been involved with the children until now, insists upon imbalanced amounts of time, or communicates to the court that they would be happy to keep the children away from the other parent.

- Each parent's stories about child sharing or parenting concerns do not match. It is a "he said/she said" argument, making it difficult to determine who is telling the truth.

- The case has earned a negative reputation with the courts because of continuous and/or frivolous litigation, as well as frequent changes in attorneys/proper representation.

- Excessive court filings, or the parents have attended several Family Court Services (FCS) appointments and continue to argue about basic child sharing issues or custody.

Scary, isn't it?

Factors that Influence High Conflict

Here are some of the factors that influence high conflict:

Fear
* of being alone
* of not having enough
* of the unknown future
* of the other parent not keeping the children safe (they are not a good parent)

Control
* to manipulate
* to not feel out of control
* the situation to feel safe
* to keep the children safe

Revenge
* "You left and now you will pay."
* "Because of all you did wrong in the marriage."
* "Because of all I gave up for the marriage."

Money
* "I worked and all you did was stay home: the money should be mine"
* "I gave up my future to take care of the family: you owe me"
* "I have all the brains: you just came along for the ride"
* "You have to continue to take care of me because you said you would"
* "It's because of all my hard work that we have money; go to work and make your own money"

Personality & Mood Disorders
* Borderline
* Narcissistic
* Bipolar
* Histrionic

Addictions
* Prescription drugs
* Street drugs
* Pornography
* Alcohol

Statistics

According to research, as many as 30% of divorcing couples will be in a high conflict divorce. Of that population, 70% will be involved with a partner who has a high conflict personality and who will strive to keep the couple entangled in conflict. In the United States in 2010 there were 1.96 million divorces. With these statistics we can calculate the following facts:

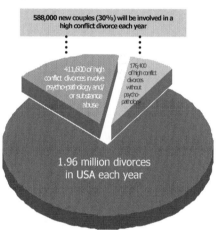

Of the 588,000, 70% or 411,600 of the high conflict population will have one or both parents that have a high conflict personality (personality disorder, substance abuse problem, or both).

The number of parents involved in high conflict divorce in the court system rises exponentially each year because most of the cases continue on unchecked for many years, causing greater and greater strain on the legal system.

588,000 new couples (30%) will be involved in a high conflict divorce each year

411,600 of high conflict divorces involve psycho-pathology and/or substance abuse

176,400 of high conflict divorces without psycho-pathology

1.96 million divorces in USA each year

People displaying high conflict personality traits tend to view relationships from a rigid and adversarial perspective. People with these traits naturally find themselves in the adversarial environment of the court system. Most of the cases that are unable to find resolution are those involving high conflict personalities.

Psychological and Physiological Causes of High Conflict

Psychological

An individual with a high conflict personality will show one or more of the following traits. Are any of these traits apparent in your situation?

- ☐ Wide mood swings
- ☐ Likely to make false statements
- ☐ Tends towards black and white thinking (things are all good or all bad)
- ☐ Perceptions of victimization followed by intense anger
- ☐ Idealization followed by devaluation of a partner or other relationship
- ☐ Presents self as invulnerable, detached
- ☐ Intense anger, even at benign events
- ☐ Believes he/she is very superior
- ☐ Preoccupation with self to the exclusion of others
- ☐ Feels entitled to special treatment
- ☐ Exhibits little empathy toward others
- ☐ Shows disregard for the rules

People with high conflict personalities are very good at the adversarial process. Their conviction and dedication to their cause can be very persuasive to inexperienced professionals including counselors, attorneys and family court services mediators.

Physiological

Conflict can be physically addictive. Adrenaline and other chemicals that are produced by the body and that control the excitation of the flight/fight response can give a sense of excitement and even enjoyment. Over a long period of time this process can become addictive. Do you know anyone who is always in conflict somewhere in his or her life? Anyone who is a drama queen/king? Have you ever seen someone who actually seems to smile and get charged up when they are in a fight? These are likely people that have high conflict personalities. The conflict cycle has gone on for much of their lives and they have not only become addicted to it, but they are also masters at keeping the conflict going. They wouldn't know what to do if they weren't in some form of turmoil.

There are two participants in this dance of conflict. The natural defensive responses we all display when we are under attack are the very responses that keep the dance going, which means we are quite likely (unwittingly) keeping the conflict cycle alive.

By disengaging from the conflict and not responding to the constant onslaught of threats and breaking of boundaries, we will break the pattern of the dance, and the conflict will be unable to continue.

During the 12-week High Conflict Diversion Program™ that I teach, there is one comment that almost all the parents make on their exit interview: How liberating it is to feel that they don't have to respond to everything the other parent throws their way. If they had only understood earlier that they didn't need to constantly defend against allegations levied against them by the other parent, they feel the conflict would have been much more manageable.

One evening before class, I was sitting and listening to the parents chat and tell stories about the other parent in their lives. Many of the conversations were about things they had done to either frustrate or mess with the other parent outright; things they had done that would anger the other parent and cause them to spin. The group as a whole laughed, and had a great time exchanging anecdotes about their cleverness.

I took this opportunity to engage in the laughter and their clear joy in upsetting the other parent. Just about everyone had done something to mess with the other parent (including yours truly, back in the day). Then I stopped abruptly and got very serious. I looked at each one of them directly and said, "What is it that each of you expect to come from this? Do you expect that this will cause the other parent to stop and think about what their next interaction with you will be? Do you think it will cause them to be more friendly? Or, do you think it will anger them and that they will come back at you with even more venom? Oh, and by the way—what about the environment you are creating for your children while they are in the other parent's house? Is it going to be easier for them to be with a parent that is triggered and angry?"

The energy of the room shifted dramatically as they began to understand how their behaviors affected and fed the ongoing conflict, and ultimately, the negative impact it had on their children.

This ended up being one of the most powerful and transformational conversations in any of my classes. As you read this, take a few minutes to sit with the feelings that arise as you ponder how you might be engaging in similar behaviors. If you are willing to do this prior to taking similar actions, my guess is that you will make a decision to do something else in the future.

"I am responsible. Although I may not be able to prevent the worst from happening, I am responsible for my attitude toward the inevitable misfortunes that darken life.

Bad things do happen; how I respond to them defines my character and the quality of my life. I can choose to sit in perpetual sadness, immobilized by the gravity of my loss, or I can choose to rise from the pain and treasure the most precious gift I have - life itself".

-- **Walter Anderson**
(Writer, 1885 - 1962)

Chapter 2

The Divorce Process

Coming to the end of a relationship is an emotional process, perhaps one of the most difficult in our life, regardless of whether we are the one leaving or the one left behind. Ultimately, separation from the other parent means that we will be traveling a different path along a different time line.

The time after a divorce or separation from the other parent can be a time of great transformation and freedom. The realization that we are no longer under the influence of our ex can have a strong positive effect on our own sense of control.

Our beliefs create our reality. The thoughts we select during this time will either free us from the conflict or keep us enmeshed with the other parent, so it is important to begin to completely take charge of them.

It is very important to think of the time after divorce as our golden opportunity to fully engage in our future. In order to make a fresh start and to have a life free of those things that caused us to divorce in the first place, we must engage in a new way of thinking. This isn't a stagnant process; it requires that we take action that under less trying circumstances we might not ever engage in. Chances are we find ourselves lost in many aspects of our life; this is the optimum time to begin to examine many things we want to change.

This is a good time to begin doing some personal work with either a therapist or life coach. You may want to go back to school or change jobs. These thoughts may seem overwhelming, so don't think you have to take them on all at once, but do take time to begin to explore them. Don't let anyone tell you, not even yourself, that you can't do any of them because of your situation.

The Power of Intention

"What is it that you want to do? Where do you want to be in your life? What is the intention for change in your life?" In order to create change we have to first answer these types of questions. The future literally begins with a thought, either positive or negative.

If we take a positive thought and from this thought then produce a plan, we begin to create the future. Each plan entails a series of events that has to take place in order to manifest its completion. It is from our focus on each event, one step at a time, that we move toward the final outcome.

We are all capable of becoming and accomplishing more than we can imagine; in order to achieve this potential our thoughts must be positive ones of empowerment and independence.

On the other hand, negative thoughts tend to keep us in a state of worry and overwhelm. They may make us feel like we can't move forward, or that we're stuck in a cycle of despair. From this place we can easily get caught up defending ourselves against things that haven't yet occurred (and that may never occur). When we are in a defensive frame of mind our attention is on defending ourselves in the conflict and not on more positive avenues of self-empowerment.

Note: Positive thinking, self-empowerment and independent action sets the stage for what will become a different style of parenting (parallel parenting) that dictates that the parents don't communicate with one another except in emergencies. The essence of this new approach is that it provides a way for parents to disconnect from one another. We will take up the discussion of Parallel Parenting in greater detail in later chapters.

Although each divorce experience is unique, there is also a real commonality to the emotions and experiences of individuals who go through a similar experience. As you look at the table on the following page, identify yourself and the role you played (and perhaps continue to play) in the dynamic of your former relationship. Let's take a brief look at these with the intention of giving ourselves a broader perspective on the entire experience of divorce.

The One Who Left

- Doubt
- Vacillation and indecision
- Resentment
- Anger, sadness, mourns the loss of a dream
- Fear/Anxiety
- Denial of the reality of the relationship
- Withdrawal
- Bargaining to change the relationship
- Guilt
- Depression
- Shattered hopes and dreams
- Resignation

The One Left Behind

- Anxiety
- A sense of something being amiss
- Fear and confusion
- Strong need for reassurance from partner
- Denial of the situation
- Bargaining to regain the relationship
- Depression
- Loss of stability, sense of failure and guilt
- Desire for retribution and revenge
- Need for compensation
- Resignation
- Shock and pain
- Denial of the reality of the breakup
- Separation distress
- Loss of attachment, disrupted sleep, inability to concentrate
- Anger / rage
- Disorientation to identity as a single person
- Sadness and despair
- Disillusionment
- Fear
- Loss of trust

The Breakup / The Announcement

- Separation euphoria
- Guilt
- Shame
- Fear of repeated failure
- Continued feelings of grief and loss
- Disorientation related to identity shift

As Time Passes...

- More stability
- Peace of mind
- Acceptance and serenity

And Much Later...

- Acceptance and Serenity

Undoubtedly, you were able to identify the roles that you and your former partner have played in the divorcing couple dynamic. What we need to do now is take a hard look at what generated and anchored the high conflict dynamics that have taken place between the two of you. Let's also find out what needs to be done to get to *acceptance and serenity*, that state that allows you to move self-reliantly and solidly forward in the knowledge that **you** are in charge of your future.

Assessing the Conflict

In order to move forward with resolution of the high conflict cycle, we must begin by understanding how the cause (or causes) of the conflict are perceived. In this part of the chapter we look at the primary "hot buttons" that come up between divorcing couples, as well as those involved in a custody fight. You will learn to tune into and identify the key issues that anchor the entire conflict between you and your ex/the other parent. We will examine the fears and emotions at the root of the conflict, and we will see how these fears and emotions give rise to finger-pointing statements assigning all of the blame to "the ex." Finally, we will see how, when we buy into those beliefs, the conflict is locked in place and goes on… and on… and on.

Fear

Fear is an energy, a recurrent theme, and a major impetus that has been with us all of our lives. Unfortunately, we are taught in our culture that fear is a viable motivator. When we look at fear as a motivator in divorce and custody issues, we see the following dynamics:

fear of letting go of the other person;
of being alone;

that the dreams you had as a couple will never be
 fulfilled;
of not being able to find another partner;
of inadequacy or not being able to manage alone;
of not having enough, and;
as odd as it sounds, fear of success.

*Food for thought: what would happen if you were able
to become completely financially independent or
completely free of your ex/ the other parent's influence?*

The biggest downside to fear is that it keeps us frozen
in old patterns. Although these fears can be overwhelming,
taking the time to identify our fears can give us a welcome
perspective on what is actually happening in the moment.

These common fears are powerful forces in preventing
individuals from detaching from their partner, accepting
the end of the relationship, and moving on. One of the
most valuable gifts we can give ourselves is to work with a
therapist or coach who can be of great help and support. A
good, experienced therapist or coach will provide many
skills to help separate the "emotion" from the "business"
of the divorce.

Much of the fear that comes up in divorce (or any
other form of conflict, for that matter) is fear of what will
happen if we don't engage in the fight or somehow react to
refute the allegations made against us. The belief is, "If I
don't defend myself, then people will believe the
allegations are true."

Control

Control is a huge issue in the dynamic of high conflict
divorces. Control is the issue that often overlaps all of the
others. It would be ideal if every individual involved in a
high conflict divorce could be made to realize early on in
the process what can and cannot be controlled. But it is the
nature of high conflict divorce to deflect our attention to

"scoring a win" by making the other person wrong, rather than acknowledging what is true. **Simply put, we need to understand what is in our control and what is not.**

There is no better time than the present to ask ourselves the most emotionally pressing question of all, and the one that is really the bottom line for all of us: Where do we feel that we are losing, have lost, or may soon lose CONTROL? (Really take the time to search for the answer. Don't skip over this!) Ask yourself, "Where do I really have control in my family life? There is only one true answer. You have control ONLY in the choices you make, and about the parenting you do in your home. You do NOT have control of your ex, the choices they make, their attitude or their behavior. You don't get to control their way of parenting or what happens in their home. You have control only over your parenting in your home. You have control over the rules that apply in your home and over the activities that you deem to be safe. You don't have any control over those issues in your ex's/the other parent's house.

Coming to an understanding of what is and what isn't in your control is essential to changing the high conflict dynamic. And then there is the challenge of getting real about the process you're involved in. Because you are involved in the court system, some form of surrender to that process is required in order for you to get on with your life.

You do not have control over your children's welfare when they are in the other parent's home. However, if you do have concern for their safety, you can educate them so they can be safer when they are not with you. Teaching children about safety is something all parents should do to empower their children. Taking responsibility to educate your children will give you the sense that things will be all right whenever they are away from you, allowing you to get on with your life and not be pre-occupied with worry. Understand that there is a time to call 9-1-1 or to take your child to the doctor because of something that needs immediate attention. Of course, if that moment arrives you need to take action.

Revenge

Another factor we will examine that drives high conflict divorce is *revenge*. The desire for revenge develops out of a victim mentality, and is based on the belief that the other person has done something unjust to us and that we must make them pay. Revenge develops out of a sense of anger, betrayal, and hurt. Behaving like the righteous victim who believes they are entitled to exact retribution will keep us stuck in the court system. It will drain all of our resources, poison our relationship with our children, and destroy our future.

The victim seeks to validate their feelings of fury, frustration and fear by laying all the blame on the other person. But the victim approach gets us nowhere. The only way to move forward is to finally come to terms with and accept "what is." First, that means that we need to accept that the person we were with is no longer (or never was) who we thought they were. By recognizing that the other person is truly not the person we want to be with any longer means that we are making a pro-active, responsible, self-loving choice for ourselves.

None of what we are dealing with has to do with the other person's behavior, as much as how we choose to deal with the behavior and then solving the accompanying problems. If the approach we take is to solve the <u>problem</u> it takes us away from feeling frozen as a victim and creates an active role that can change the outcome of this most difficult time. Solve the problem at hand and move on.

Money

When I was growing up my father would use the expression *"a dollar chasing after a dime."* It aptly describes the dynamics of so many high conflict cases. The real price that is paid by the parties in high conflict cases is huge and so often goes unrecognized. There are very real costs in terms of each person's emotional energy, their time and the often exorbitant attorney's fees that are paid. And in so many high conflict cases these costs are repeated again and again as the individuals involved keep using the same methods to try to get a different outcome.

It is my experience that when the resources for "the fight" have been diminished by escalating attorney's fees and court costs, the individuals involved (i.e., the warring ex's/parents) discover previously unrecognized abilities within themselves, manage to create new life strategies, and find or generate the money they need in order to make it all work.

The topic of money can be an enormous source of conflict involving many issues with underlying emotional charges. There may be anxiety about getting your fair share for everything you did in the marriage. There may be anger that is expressed by wanting to punish the other parent by withholding and controlling money for as long as possible to make them suffer for all the bad things you perceive that they did to you during the marriage, or for the hurt and pain they caused you when they left. The conflict around money can also stem from fears about survival. These can become obsessive thoughts about not having enough money, and thinking that you have to continue to depend on your ex/the other parent to provide for you for your continued survival.

Another tell-tale sign that the nature of the conflict is money-centric is when statements like the following are made: "You didn't contribute to the family," or "I earned all the money," or "You don't deserve help because you really don't do anything—you're just lazy." These statements may be indicators that there is a real imbalance in the couple's power structure. These attitudes also allude to individuals with control issues. The relationship dynamics would then need to be dealt with from that perspective.

When money and fear mix, the combination can be like flypaper—keeping you stuck and entangled with your ex in a way that doesn't allow you to move on and embrace your own future. When you are tethered to a person who is no longer a part of your life you are anchored to the past. This restricts the possibilities of what your future can be.

Money and the Children

When money is a point of contention it can show up in several ways. Often, one of the parents will ask for a 50% child time-share even when their work schedule will ultimately not support this. They will try for this custody arrangement even though it may not be in the best interests of the children, and even though they haven't previously made the effort to spend large blocks of time parenting their children when the time <u>was</u> available to them. Under these circumstances the request for a 50% child time-share can be a red flag revealing that the underlying conflict is financially based.

Another way this money issue can be expressed is when the other parent fears that income is being falsely reported or hidden because one of the parents is self-employed or has investments. The fight continues as one person tries to prove that the other parent isn't giving their fair share for child or spousal support. It is critical to understand that, in this scenario, great amounts of time and money can be spent trying to uncover "hidden" money. Sometimes these efforts fail completely.

In the meantime, what about the children? In spite of the fact that the "children's welfare" might be a key point of disagreement between you and your ex, what may be overlooked is that the current needs of your children are not being met. When you and your ex are spending time and resources on the conflict, your attention is on the fight, not on your children. Although your stated intentions are that you are doing this for the good of the children, the reality is that they are not benefiting. Furthermore, there is a good chance that if you were to look long and hard at the situation you might well find that the ongoing conflict is being fueled by one or more of the factors mentioned above.

Fear, resentment and an insistence that justice be served are emotions that underlie such statements as "the other parent makes plenty of money and they are depriving me of my share" or, "It's not for me, it's for the kids." I then ask to see if there is another way to solve the problem that doesn't include the cooperation of the other parent. Inevitably, the discussion produces several options that don't require the other parent's participation and a shift occurs in the parent's belief about needing that help.

Money may indeed be an issue, but *the charge* behind these communications is an emotional one. These statements resonate with a sense of victimhood disguised as an issue of fairness and/or a fear of not having enough. The statement, "It's for the kids" is often a smokescreen that covers up the fact that there is some underlying justification for one's behavior.

Coming to terms with this idea could create a real turning point for you and your children. It would help you see that the battle you've been waging is not in the best interests of your children and that you can, in fact, make it without the money you've been fighting for; you know this because you have been able to make it so far. This may be a reach for many of you, but just coming to terms with this idea is enough to help ease up on some of the fight.

Further, by letting go of the fight you free yourself to move into other endeavors, maybe including a new career that empowers you to break fully away from your ex and start living life the way you choose to.

Of course you should work toward an equitable settlement. However, your ability to expand your current circumstances is in your control—and no one else's. It is critical that you learn when it is in your and your children's best interests to disengage from the other parent enough to stop the high conflict cycle. Only then can you take control of the future for both of you.

Personality Disorders

Recent studies show that one in five people in the U.S. have a diagnosable Personality Disorder (PD)[iii]. These PDs frequently lie at the core of the personalities found in family court and that drive high conflict cases. Study of this population indicates that as much as 20% of high conflict cases involve a PD in one or both parents, or some form of addiction (frequently these two go hand in hand).[iv] Herein lies the problem: most court officials (judges and attorneys) don't understand PDs—how people with a personality disorder behave and what is at the core of their behavior. Additionally, many mental health professionals don't understand PDs either because they haven't spent a lot of time working with this population. (The reason for this is that most of this population doesn't self-refer—they seem fine to themselves!) The truth of the matter is that this population is not going to change their behavior under any situation; they will constantly break rules or stretch them to a point that they may as well have been broken. This behavior will keep you (and your children) in constant chaos and turmoil.

"Everyone has a responsibility to not only tolerate another person's point of view, but also to accept it eagerly as a challenge to your own understanding. And express those challenges in terms of serving other people."

-- Arlo Guthrie
(American folk singer, 1947 -   )

Chapter 3

Examining Beliefs

"As long as you have certain desires about how it ought to be you can't see how it is."
— Ram Dass: Spiritual Teacher

Accepting our situation and losing the idealized concept of how we thought it was opens doors to solving problems. This entails taking responsibility for our role in the breakdown of the relationship. We need to come to the realization at some point that we have at least 50% of the responsibility for the conflict—that we made choices along the way that landed us in this spot. By not accepting our situation, we are unable to take appropriate action—because we are responding to something that doesn't exist.

Here are examples of the mindset that may have contributed to our situation:

~ We ignored signs early in the relationship of the other
person's violent behavior, convinced that we could
change this person;

~ We thought we could "save" them;

~ We reconciled ourselves to lies, secrets, or any number
of behaviors that were inappropriate, and/or excused
our own inappropriate communications and behaviors.

Taking responsibility for missing these red flags will
help us let go of heavy emotional baggage—such as
frustration, anger and a desire for revenge—that would
otherwise continue to poison us, our children, and the
future we desire to create with them.

Accepting "what is" means that we decide to take
100% responsibility for all the choices we make from this
point forward, regardless of what the other person says or
does. We let go of all attachment to the other person and
what they think in order to move forward into a richer and
more productive life—in which we create the shape of our
future.

Creation of Space

Very few couples that split up or divorce agree about
anything at all, especially parenting. In the beginning,
most of the arguing and fighting is over anything and
everything. The separation process is incomplete and
emotions are raw. Every time these people are in contact
with one another a squabble breaks out and often escalates
into a full-on argument; this behavior is an extension of
the differences and arguments they had as a couple. There
is no reason to think that this is going to stop now that the
situation has changed.

At the very least, the structure of this behavior needs
to be broken down before a new structure can be built on a
healthier foundation. This behavior has to have strong
boundaries instilled around it so it doesn't leak out and

constantly affect the children caught in the middle.

Continued conflict is a sentence of psychological instability and constant pain for both you and the children. It doesn't have to be this way. Children of warring parents are often happy to see their parents split up because they believe the fighting will stop. The problem is the fighting doesn't stop, it simply takes on a new venue (Family Court), with the children still caught in the middle.

It has been proven over and over again that in high conflict divorces co-parenting rarely works. Being told to co-parent with the person with whom you're in intense conflict can leave you feeling hopelessly trapped.

Without the structure of a good parenting plan (which will be discussed in a later chapter), the arena is left wide open for misbehavior by one or both parents. It becomes easy to keep the children from seeing the other parent, or to hold that parent hostage by withholding visitation. The faster that formal boundaries are established the better.

High conflict couples CAN'T co-parent. When forced to try, co-parenting only makes the situation worse. There is an answer. This concept is gaining recognition as a viable alternative to the co-parenting model, and is called *Parallel Parenting*.

Parallel parenting creates the structure and boundaries needed to stop, or at the very least manage, the high conflict cycle. This model of parenting gives each parent' autonomy over their respective homes. The children adapt to different rules in each home. Each parent leaves the other to parent the way that parent wants, whether or not they agree with that parenting style. The lines of communication (phone, face-to-face meeting) are eliminated, and the only forms of communication take place in writing by email, text (in emergency), or fax. This keeps the possibility of misunderstanding or miscommunication to a minimum. Phone calls to the children when with the other parent are minimized, giving each parent a greater sense of autonomy.

Exchanges or transitions are minimized so the children have an opportunity to settle in to one home for a time, while keeping contact between the parents required for exchanges to a minimum. Exchanges are done at school/daycare or with a neutral third party. Used in conjunction with a precise and well-written parenting plan, you have the beginning of a good management plan for the high conflict couple.

The interesting thing about parallel parenting is that the model works very well with parents that are in moderate to low conflict divorces as well. In order to move on with their lives and process their anger or disappointment over the break up, what they need most is space. If given that space the healing happens more quickly and the parents of this group are able to come into a co-parenting relationship, which is the optimum relationship for the children.

An Ounce of Prevention…

When high conflict behavior is either ignored or not identified, you have problems. Given proper structure, disengagement boundaries and consequences for improper behavior, these cases can be managed—especially when interventions happen early.

If there is a history of behavior, such as filing for a temporary restraining order over false allegations, for example, it is likely to happen again—but next time you may be set up in a way that puts you in a precarious position, making it look like something is happening that is not. This happens because you engaged in a way that left you exposed.

Here is an example of what can happen:

Tom came into my office one morning after spending the weekend in jail. He was extremely emotional and confused about what to do next. It seems that on the previous Friday evening he had come home from work and was sitting on the couch at his ex-wife's house waiting to pick up his children when the doorbell rang. When he answered it, there were two police officers who proceeded to tell him they had received a domestic violence call. Just then his wife came into the room crying, showing the police a recent self-inflicted bruise. The police then arrested Tom and he spent the next two days in jail. Mom subsequently filed and was granted a temporary restraining order so Tom wasn't able to see his children for three weeks. When he was able to see them it was with supervised visitation, and under the condition that he take an anger management class, a high conflict parenting class and a regular parenting class. This process took more than three months, after which it took another six months to get back to a normal schedule with his children.

I can't tell you how many times I have heard this and other stories like it. If a situation arises where, even remotely, you could be set up, don't go near it. If you can think it, it can and will happen. Be prepared.

"Most people do not really want freedom,
because freedom involves
responsibility, and most people are frightened of
responsibility."

-- Sigmund Freud
(Father of Psychoanalysis, 1858 - 1939)

Chapter 4

Conflict and the Court System

There are a number of incorrect beliefs and basic misunderstandings about how the court system works, all of which perpetuate our fears about divorce. One of these beliefs is that if we don't do things in just a certain way we will be seen as bad or unworthy, and could lose our children.

Another false assumption is that we have to respond to any and every allegation made by the other party, or the court will assume these allegations to be true. Yet another is that the court will make the other parent follow the rules: s/he will be held in contempt of court or punished in some way for her/his misbehavior. **None of these is true.**

Furthermore, there is a whole host of other erroneous beliefs about what the court system will do. It is important to recognize that these false assumptions play a large part in keeping the conflict going because each of the parties involved feels like they have a chance of winning, i.e. being proved "right" and the other person proved "wrong."

The realization of what is in our control and what is not is an essential part of coming to terms with our reality. Start by asking yourself these questions: "What has been working for me, and what hasn't?", "What am I sacrificing by continuing to battle with my ex?" We must answer these questions in light of the fact that the further we get into the court system the less control we have over our own lives.

Knowing how the family court system works and how it tends to decide cases can help alleviate many of the fears that crop up during the divorce and custody process. In my opinion, it is essential to consult with people who have had personal experiences of the court system. Ask them how the judicial system worked for them and how it affected their lives—especially in ways they did not bargain for.

The crucial question to be asking is, "Are my expectations of the outcome realistic?" I often find that people have no idea what to expect and that nobody prepares them for what is to come. This lack of preparedness leads to a heightened sense of anxiety as well as feeling (once again) a lack of control.

As you enter the family court system, if you are unable to reach agreements with the other parent about child custody, you will be giving your decision-making power to someone else; someone who knows little about your situation—someone who will be making decisions for your child until your child is eighteen.

In my experience, many divorce attorneys take charge without explaining the process, or what is going to happen. Then they let us know (in no uncertain terms) that they are "in charge" and that we just need to let them do their job. This approach by attorneys often makes us (their clients) more afraid of doing the wrong thing. Under this duress, it is no wonder that our solutions may never be explored.

Instead of having our attorney "take charge," what we

really need is to be empowered to be part of the process, and encouraged to participate in a knowledgeable manner to move the conflict toward a successful, solution-driven outcome.

After gathering all of the information you need to understand what is to come, take time to work out a plan of what it is you want as the outcome, and take an active role in directing your attorney to that end.

Understanding the Court System and High Conflict Divorce

The courts see thousands of people in high conflict divorce each year. They don't have the resources to deal with ongoing court appearances by these conflicted couples. After brief encounters, the court has to make judgments on what is going on with these people in the course of a couple of hours.

Expectations for what the court can/should do causes the conflict to continue on and on. Cases are prolonged at the high cost of court time, parent time, court and attorney fees, and—most importantly—continued damage to the children.

Decisions made in family court are what the court perceives to be in the "best interests of the child." Many of the determinations are made without proper or accurate information. The court system doesn't have the resources to properly investigate the allegations of every feuding couple that comes to them, nor do many of the professionals within the court system have any experience in dealing with high conflict personalities.

Perjury in Family Court (in most states) is not something that is prosecuted or even investigated. Because people in family court lie all the time, it is hard for the court to figure out what is actually true in order to make a good determination.

Actions taken by one or the other parent are of little or no concern to the court. However, one parent might keep trying to get the court to "make" the other parent do something differently (e.g., force the other parent to make the children call at a particular time, or require the other parent to be on time to pick-up or drop off the children, etc.).

Here is an example of one such conflict:

John and Kimberly had been divorced for two years. They had two young boys, Jack (8) and Billy (10), and there seemed to be little problem between them until Kimberly got a new boyfriend and began taking the boys out to the desert. They rode quad-runners and motorcycles on her weekends with the boys. John was outraged that Kim would allow their children to engage in such a dangerous activity and began trying to block these activities and take time away from her because she was obviously a bad parent who couldn't make appropriate decisions regarding the safety of the children.

When John went to family court over the issue the court made no change. John was further outraged at the system for not seeing how dangerous this situation was to the children. For the next year John was continually trying to find ways to make Kim stop this "outrageous activity with his children" by calling her, showing up late with the children for exchanges, and telling the children what a terrible parent their mother was. Soon the court began to take time away from John for his behavior, which further infuriated him.

John was ordered to a High Conflict Diversion Program™ class. After hearing John's story we suggested that he try something different. We suggested he take his boys to an off-road motorcycle safety school that would teach the boys all the appropriate safety techniques and all about the necessary safety gear. John's response was that he thought we were nuts. He assured us that this was out of the question because surely we could see how dangerous and inappropriate this activity was for kids his children's age!

Two weeks went by. When John next came to class we asked him what was happening with his problem regarding his ex-wife and his children's safety. It seems that John had taken our advice after all. He started taking the children to a safety class at one of the off-road riding schools in the area, and John decided to take the class with his boys. Now he goes riding with them on his time, he no longer bothers Kim about their trips to the desert with the children, and he even supports one of the boys riding in competition motocross.

In this story, John hadn't let go of the relationship with his ex, as evidenced by what seemed to be a working co-parenting relationship. By working closely with the mother he was able to stay close and maintain a relationship with her. This all looked and felt like a healthy co-parenting set-up.

Perspective

After hearing all of the declarations and depositions, and after handing down all of their stipulations and subpoenas, family courts in many states tend to lean toward giving both parents equal time with their children.

When all is said and done, fighting it out in court over the many little things (which is, believe it or not, what most of the conflicts are about) accomplishes little beyond causing further harm to the children, depleting the family estate, putting money in the attorneys' pockets, and keeping the parties involved from moving on and finding joy in their lives. *I have never seen the court process solve a high conflict custody matter. It always comes from the parent's willingness to change or for one parent to decide to totally disengage from the fight.*

Let's put this all into perspective. We are here on this earth for such a short time. The possibilities afforded us in this life are nothing short of incredible when we choose to take advantage of them. To spend any portion of our time caught up in a fight that, in most cases, is by definition unwinnable, is a waste. It is a waste of our life, our children's lives and their emotional well-being, which is our responsibility to care for and enhance.

"A quarrel is quickly settled when deserted by one party; there is no battle unless there be two."

--Lucius Annaeus Seneca
(Roman philosopher and playwright, 4 BC - 65 AD)

Chapter 5

Contact Equals Conflict

If you find yourself in a high conflict custody battle, every time you engage with your ex/the other parent and argue about any of the many things the two of you fight about, you add energy to the fight and perpetuate the conflict. No matter how you approach a conversation, your experience is likely to be one of conflict.

The question then becomes, how do you **manage** this ongoing situation (note that I didn't use the word control)? You manage the situation by not engaging in the conflict. You pull your energy away from the fight and disengage from having contact with your ex/the other parent. You then set up boundaries that keep that person from disrupting your household. For example, you parent independently and cooperatively, not in an adversarial manner. What you're doing is focusing on your own world; "This is my world. This is the way I do it."

When we enter into an adversarial position, there's always a loser. That is what our judicial system and family courts are based on and how attorneys view our situation. The attorneys go in to win or lose. This does not have to be about winning or losing. Our children lose if we stay in conflict. If that means that we give up one day of custody a week to make it easier for the kids, then we have to (at least) explore the option.

If the root of the conflict is about money, find another way. It's an abundant universe. In almost all of the cases I have been involved with, the parent manages to make their financial situation work without the other parent. One way or another, the children are provided with the essentials needed for their well-being. Sometimes you have to adjust your lifestyle. Downscale. Get simple. We've been running amok in this country for the last 30 years because we've tried to live far beyond what we can realistically sustain. It's important to teach our children a different way of living so they don't make the same mistakes.

Parenting

In a divorce where children are involved, co-parenting is the ideal approach. Co-parenting in a low conflict divorce allows for the ability of BOTH parents to allow the other to parent.

In a high conflict divorce, typically one or both of the parents try to control how the children are raised and may find it difficult to trust the other parent's ability to make good decisions concerning the children. The children become objects to be fought over, causing their needs to become secondary to the fight.

However, the reality of the situation is that there are different rules a child has to follow in each of their parent's homes. Each home will have different rules. It's important for each parent to trust that the other parent is competent to make good decisions and be willing to talk with the children about what is going on in the children's world.

The cooperative piece comes in because you're not

pushing the other person's buttons. You're not trying to bend them to do something differently. Regardless of how they parent, you accept how they parent by understanding what's driving their parenting model and understanding that you have no dominion over it.

If you try to impose your will on them, they are going to fight you. Instead, if you can say, "Okay. I understand where they're coming from and the core issues that are driving them," then you can also give the children a buffer from the conflict by modeling the skill of dealing with that personality type.

We have to challenge ourselves by respectfully and consistently setting good boundaries. Saying, "That behavior doesn't work for me", allows us to disengage from the situation entirely rather than engage in conflict. The boundary setting piece we are modeling for our children is the skill set they need in order to learn to deal with conflict in a healthy and appropriate manner. By managing the conflict this way, we are teaching our children how to negotiate in conflicted situations, or at the very least, manage themselves in a way in which they don't find themselves constantly drawn into conflict.

We have to parent as if the other parent doesn't exist; not out of disrespect or malice, but out of the need to disengage from the argument and have the energy of the fight dissipate. We have to give our children whatever they need, irrespective of the other parent's willingness or ability to do the same. If we parent from that perspective, we will thrive, as will our children. Our children are going to see the model of what it's like to take charge of their own lives and take care of themselves. They don't grow up with the idea that someone else is responsible, so the idea of being a victim never occurs to them.

Instead of saying, "So, I should do nothing, then. I shouldn't go to court to get that daycare money. I just pay on my own," say, "Okay, no matter what happens, I'm going to do the right thing." The right thing is not about teaching the other parent a lesson. The right thing is about doing what's right for our children. Our children need new shoes. Our children need books. Our children need a new bike. Our children need an education. Most importantly: Our children need to see us modeling "do the right thing" behavior. If we don't do this, the children will be the only losers, caught once again in the middle.

Contact Equals Stress

When we see, speak to, or even think about a person who makes us feel stressed, that stress produces a biochemical reaction in our brains. It can take days to completely return to the pre-stress state. For example, stress can take a real toll on mood and sleep patterns. Surely, you can relate to this.

In addition, there are several other physiological consequences of stress on the body that we may be less aware of, but that are equally significant. And even though this is not a biology or physiology class, let's take a moment and look at the major physiological consequences of stress. You may find it quite enlightening!

Our bodies respond to stress in different ways, depending on the degree and duration of the stress. Short-term stress sends us into the well-known "fight or flight" response. (Think of caveman running away from angry saber-tooth tiger as fast as his legs can carry him.) The body produces adrenaline, which in turn raises our heart rate, increases our blood pressure and tells the liver to release sugar, all in preparation for dealing with a dangerous situation. When the crisis is over the adrenaline subsides. This is the survival mechanism that is the up side of "fight or flight".

Short-term stress also has its down-side, however. In addition to adrenaline, the adrenal glands secrete cortisol. Cortisol sends messages to our metabolism that we might not choose for ourselves, like breaking down body protein (muscle) for fuel, the laying down of abdominal fat, disturbance of blood sugar levels and decrease in thyroid function.

Then there is long-term stress. Long-term stress (such as the stress of ongoing relationship conflicts) produces abnormal cortisol levels in the body and eventually weakens the stress response system. Cortisol suppresses inflammation and dissolves connective tissue. (This is why cortisone, a synthetic version of cortisol, is used to melt old scar tissue or reduce local inflammation.) Sustained cortisol production causes higher blood pressure and an increase in the body's abdominal fat. This is the fat that is highly associated with "bad" (LDL) cholesterol and less "good" (HDL) cholesterol, as well as heart attacks and strokes. As if that weren't enough, there's also a weakening of the musculoskeletal system, a general lowering of immunity, slower wound healing, and impaired cognitive function. Phew! Long-term stress is implicated in many common chronic diseases, such as chronic fatigue syndrome, anxiety disorders, eating disorders, fibromyalgia, and depression, just to mention a few.

Here's how long-term stress applies very specifically to parents: We have observed that each time parents in a high conflict divorce have contact there is nervous system activation that lasts about **72 hours**. This cycle starts with anticipation of the exchange of the children, the event itself, and the time it takes to return to the smooth routine of being with the children. That means that you are experiencing a lot of stress over and above the general stresses of life that everyone experiences.

Given these facts, the question you need to start asking is this: "Can I do anything to decrease my stress levels when it comes to having contact with my ex?" The answer to that question is a resounding "Yes!" The next question, of course, is "What can I do?" The answer is to create and enforce boundaries. Practice parallel parenting. Create a solid parenting plan, as we'll discuss in a later chapter.

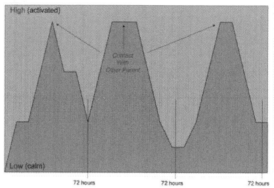

"If it's never our fault, we can't take responsibility for it. If we can't take responsibility for it, we'll always be its victim."

-- Richard Bach
(Author, *Jonathan Livingston Seagull*, 1936 -   )

Chapter 6

Parallel Parenting vs. Co-parenting

Parallel parenting is a way of parenting in which the parents agree to parent in their own styles; i.e. they don't try to agree on a single set of rules for raising the children. They understand that trying to do so only causes problems between them. Each parent can have differing skills and still parent their children effectively. The goal of parallel parenting is for **you** to do the best job you can during the time you are with your children.

Children are capable of adjusting to two different sets of rules and parenting styles. In fact, making this adjustment is easier on them than having two parents who are constantly trying to make each other do it "their way." We know that children can make this adjustment because they have different teachers, coaches and other authority figures during the course of their day. In most cases, they adapt to the differences in teaching styles, rules and expectations.

Research has shown us that cooperative parenting creates the best outcome for children of divorce, and that conflicted parenting has the worst outcome for children of divorce. We also know that forcing parents into co-parenting when they are incapable of doing so only creates more conflict.

Parallel parenting becomes the optimal style of parenting when it's been determined that you cannot cooperatively parent because you find yourself in a high conflict divorce or custody fight. Disengagement is the foundation required for parallel parenting. To disengage means that you avoid contact with the other parent so that conflict cannot develop. Richard Bach writes in Jonathan Livingston Seagull, if you don't take responsibility you will always be the victim. It is your responsibility to disengage from the conflict regardless of the other parent's actions. In order to disengage it is necessary to set strong healthy boundaries for yourself. The less contact you have with the other parent, the better.

Parallel parenting is the best parenting model for high conflict divorces because it increases autonomy, decreases contact between the parents and allows each to make their own decisions regarding the children, thus eliminating opportunity for argument. Parallel parenting doesn't require the consent of both parents to agree on the model, it only requires the setting of boundaries by one of the parents.

Boundary Setting

When you begin to set boundaries you may meet with resistance from the other parent for two main reasons: (1) because you didn't set boundaries in the past, and/or (2) because you are interacting or communicating in a manner not recognizable (and possibly perceived as threatening) to the other parent.

If boundary-setting is new to the relationship, and we allow the other parent to continue behaving in ways that upset us, the relationship may become even more difficult as the other person attempts to get us to lapse back into our old familiar behavior patterns (at first). Our family harmony may feel jeopardized as the other parent continues to act out. Regardless of their reaction, we must remain firm in our boundary setting.

How long s/he keeps up this behavior is impossible to predict. But experience shows that when we continue to set boundaries, we no longer fuel the conflict and over time it runs out of gas. Remember, we need to let go of the old conflict behaviors before the other parent will learn that we are committed to our new process. If we break down and start engaging in the conflict again during this transition time, the ex will "win." Then we will have to start the boundary setting process all over again.

You might think that parallel parenting means being uncooperative. That is a misconception, and requires a closer look. There is a wide range (from total disengagement and written-only communication to simply allowing them to parent their own way) within which parallel parenting works. Parallel parenting sets healthy boundaries for the initial conditions of the divorce or separation and keeps parents from engaging when emotions are at their highest and most volatile state. If things get better, parents naturally begin to work more closely together. If things don't progress, the children are kept from being in the middle of the parents' disagreements, as the conditions for disengagement have already been established.

Sometimes, when I present the idea of parallel parenting, a parent will argue that not keeping tabs on what is going on in the other house is irresponsible and leaves the children unprotected. My reply to that, and as discussed earlier: **we can only control what goes on in our home. The best way to do that is through connection with our children, proper modeling and**

education. If we are good parents who model positive values, what we give our children by example can be what they need to get them through to adulthood. However, if we continue to engage in conflict it is likely that they will not get the care, nurturing and modeling necessary for them to be successful in their adult life.

Here is a chart that explains the differences between co-parenting and parallel parenting:

Co-Parenting vs. Parallel Parenting

Co-Parenting

1) Focuses on the needs of the children.
2) Parents communicate often and display flexibility. They interact face-to-face; communication by phone is easy.
3) Major decisions about the child such as school, extracurricular activities, health care (for example) are discussed jointly.
4) Parents work cooperatively in order to resolve child-related issues.
5) Parents work towards agreement on what is best for the children.
6) Allows flexible transitions from one home to the other.
7) Allows for schedule change.

Parallel Parenting

1) Focuses on disengaging from contact with the other parent
2) Parents speak only in emergencies; the use of email becomes the primary conduit for exchanging information. All communication is done in writing. Text messaging can be used in emergencies.
3) Major decisions are "communicated" and the parenting plan is the guide used for determining the

outcome.

4) Mom's House/Dad's House is the rule of the day. Each parent can have different rules and are autonomous in their decision making when the children are in their care.
5) Parents may have differing opinions about what is best for the children.
6) Transitions between homes are structured and non-flexible. This allows for less chaos and anxiety for the children.
7) The parenting plan is followed exactly without offering room for any change in the schedule.

Some of the ways parents keep themselves engaged in conflict and keep their "presence" in the other parent's home are:

- Constant phone calls to criticize or to chat
- Messages delivered through the children
- Being contrary about everything that has to do with the children
- Criticizing, nagging or taking the other parent to task via email or text messages
- Trying to set the other parent up so that they look bad if co-parenting isn't done according to their rules

The saying, **"What other people think about me is none of my business,"** is the type of thinking that is needed here. Parallel parenting mitigates most of the opportunity for conflict.

In the early stages of divorce, it is normal for tensions and emotions to be high; it's more common than not. I think most everyone will agree that people need time and space to process their emotions. Finding proper ways to both contain and appropriately express their anger over the shock, feelings of betrayal and abandonment, and to get their head around what life is going to look like in the future takes work and reflection. This doesn't happen overnight.

In a high conflict divorce, it is not helpful to stay engaged with the other parent. In fact in most cases, it is critical to not engage. This is where some of us may disagree. For the sake of the children, it is important to keep tensions between the parents low. This will allow the children to adapt more quickly and easily. We must understand that each parent will find their way, and it is important for them to go through this process.

Often during the marriage, the parents had differing concepts on how to raise their children. When the divorce occurs, that split is often exacerbated. By using the basic principles of parallel parenting, a non-combative structure begins to form. Each parent feels the autonomy to raise their children in their own competent fashion. The parent that wasn't so involved, if there was one, comes to understand the need for more involvement.

Given the lack of controlling behavior and involvement from the other parent, they may begin to ask questions, creating an opening for more cooperative roles by both parents. This is a natural progression, and cannot be dictated by anyone. In the cases where this progression doesn't take place, the non-combative, disengaged structure of parallel parenting is already established and the damage done due to a high conflict parenting pattern are greatly mitigated.

Human nature is such that during a divorce, the split causes parents to become polarized and prone to outbursts of anger. This causes them to lose sight of their children's needs. Parallel parenting creates an opportunity for each parent to have the chance to focus on the needs of the children in a way that is best suited to their new circumstances.

Like us, your children are sometimes going to make mistakes and poor choices. It is your job to help them figure out, a. how to not repeat them, and b. how to learn from them. Having an open relationship with your children takes a lot of time and effort. If you are spending time focused on your battle with the other parent, your focus can't be on what is happening with your children.

Here's an example:

I had a client who had a 15-year-old daughter "Janette". When Janette was with her mother "Nancy", she would have a friend over and the mother would keep tabs on her daughter. When Janette was with her father she would (as teenagers often do) convince her father to let her go to a friend's house where there was little supervision. Dad's thinking was that supervision was taking place and all was well. Nancy would call the father, tell him what was going on and try to convince him to stop letting their daughter spend the night with that friend because she was worried that the friend was not a good influence on her daughter.

Dad took this as the Nancy's way of continuing to "go off on him", telling him what to do and complaining to him about how bad a father he was. He set his boundaries with her, telling her to stay out of his parenting time. Nancy continued to worry about their daughter and stay "worked up" about the issue, continuing to try to get the court to make changes to the parenting plan. The fight went on and on and on.

I suggested to Nancy that, in this case, the approach she was taking was a continuation of their marital dispute. Her ongoing efforts to get the court to make and enforce a change in the father's behavior were not getting her anywhere. Emotionally and financially, this approach had been both difficult and costly. I suggested that there was another approach to addressing the problem that had her so worried. First, she might consider shifting her time and energies from the court battle to her daughter—really spending quality time with Janette. And second, she could create wonderful opportunities during this mom-daughter time to share with her daughter the very values that she was concerned her daughter wasn't developing.

The plan was for Nancy to cultivate a closer relationship with Janette so that discussion—rather than anxiety and suspicion—could take place between the two of them. A couple of specific recommendations were made: (1) for Nancy to start relating to Janette as a young woman, whom she trusted to make good choices for herself, rather than as a child who needed constant supervision; (2) for Nancy to share stories about her own adolescence and about the choices she had made at that time—both good and bad—and how they had impacted her in the short and long-term. In this way, Nancy could create real "teachable moments" by simply sharing her values with Janette in story form. An added bonus would be that Janette might begin to understand something about where her mother's concerns for her came from. ("Wow! . . . My mom really was once a teenager herself!")

What happened next between Nancy and Janette was transformative for both of them. Nancy started sharing with Janette her own experiences and concerns as an adolescent. As she remembered her own experiences, insecurities and anxieties as a teen, Nancy began to create common ground for discussions with Janette. Nancy began to relate so much better to Janette that she was soon able to set aside her worrying long enough to really listen to her. And Nancy was also able to better explain to Janette about her concerns as a parent. On her part, Janette was really amazed by some of the stories Nancy "told on herself." As a result she was able to relate better to her mother and to understand why her mom seemed to be worried about her all the time. As Janette came to realize that her mother wasn't trying to keep her from having a good time but was genuinely concerned for her, Janette's behavior began to change.

Over time their relationship continued to improve.

As Nancy gave Janette more freedom to show that she could be a responsible young adult, Janette responded by acting more responsibly. Soon she was able to demonstrate to Nancy that the values her mother cared so deeply for were, in fact, now her own. And she chose to exercise them consistently in both her mother's and her father's households.

Fighting with the other parent over how to raise your children only leaves your children caught in the middle of the parental fight with no solid relationship with either parent, and no clear structure or support system to provide for their needs.

"Anxiety in children is originally nothing other than an expression of the fact they are feeling the loss of the person they love."

-- Sigmund Freud
(Father of Psychoanalysis (1856 – 1939)

Chapter 7

Mom's House | Dad's House

Children adapt to different rules and surroundings, as stated in a previous chapter. Mom's House/Dad's House is another way of looking at our separation from the other parent and creating boundaries around that separation. Children are usually extremely relieved when told they don't need to tell us what the other parent is doing or saying about us in the other house. It can be extremely freeing, as well.

Asking our children what is happening in the other home, what Dad's new girlfriend is like, or what kind of job Mom's new boyfriend has, creates great discomfort in our children and isn't fair to ask . Once again, our children feel caught in the middle, and we are creating an emotional burden for them that they are not prepared for.

Be aware, also, that children will say things that may not be true simply because they think that this is what we want to hear. What is their motivation? They're trying to take care of us and our feelings the only way they know how.

Our child may tell us that the new girlfriend or step-parent is mean because they don't want us to think that they like the new girlfriend or step-parent. They may tell us they never have fun at the other parent's house because they don't want us to think they don't miss us, or because they think it's not okay for them to have fun if we are alone—that it may make us feel bad and miss them more. Our child may tell us they don't want to go to the other parent's house out of fear of making us feel bad if they do want to go. Or they may worry that we think they love the other parent more than they love us. If they're doing this with us, they may be doing exactly the same thing with the other parent as well. There's a double whammy to this kind of behavior: it keeps them caught in the middle between their two parents, and it can also contribute to us having beliefs about the other parent that aren't true. It's a mess for everyone involved!

When parents divorce or couples separate the family structure obviously changes. It is also inevitable that the rules and culture in the new families will also change, especially when a new partner is introduced. I have heard countless times from parents that were able to co-parent just fine until a new significant other came into the picture, and then everything fell apart. There are several reasons this occurs, and it's something that we can stop. It doesn't matter whether it is our new partner or the other parent's new partner.

One type of situation that may occur when the other parent has a new relationship is that he/she begins to act differently, either by being more aggressive in their approach to issues or becoming critical of things that previously were not an issue. In this case their new partner may be feeling insecure about the good relationship we have with the other parent, or the new partner may not like the parenting style and want to interject their thoughts on the matter of parenting (this can be especially present with a blended family).

Another type of situation may occur when you have a new relationship; the ease with which you used to communicate and co-parent no longer exists and everything becomes a struggle with the other parent. This is often because the other parent hasn't let go of the relationship, even though you are no longer together. The fact that you are able to continue to talk and get along indicates to the other parent that you are still a couple; when the new partner enters the picture, the signal is that the relationship is over. The twisted side of this situation is that by creating conflict they get to maintain the relationship, albeit a conflicted one.

In either case, the prescription is the same: DISENGAGE!!! By not answering the accusations or arguing the matter, we give no energy to the fight. When faced with any form of conflict, if we don't respond it eventually goes away, as long as we can maintain a neutral attitude and not take it personally.

What Happens at the Other Parent's House Stays There

We can put an end to anyone's being caught in the middle by making an agreement with our children that we won't ask them about their time at the other parent's house. If for some reason we forget, we let them know that they are free to say "Dad, that's at Mom's house. Remember... we don't talk about that here." And if they start to tell us what went on at the other parent's house we can say to them, "That's at Mom's house and I don't want to talk about that. We are here now." The same principle applies with rules. Let's say the child is watching TV, and you say "It's time for bed." The child may reply, "At Dad's house we get to stay up until 10:00 and watch TV." Your response would be, "That's at Dad's house. Here we go to bed at 9:00 sharp, and you know that's the rule here." This creates both a valid and a valuable boundary with our children, and it keeps us from engaging in arguments with and about the other parent.

However, if conditions at the other parent's house present a real threat to the safety or well-being of our child, what then? Sometimes there is a need for action to be taken on behalf of the children. Unfortunately, since family court is so busy dealing with people who make false accusations against one another, they can be slow to listen to a parent who is actually making a valid accusation about the other parent; consequently, going to court is probably not a good choice. At those times it is critical that the children have someone to talk to who will be responsible for taking the action required.

The Importance of Having a Counselor For the Children

There are a couple of important reasons to have a counselor for our children, both during a custody battle and beyond. The first is that the children need a place to process the issues that come up for them regarding the divorce or custody issues. Just because we have been able to disengage from the fight doesn't mean the other parent is keeping the children out of it.

Secondly, as stated earlier, there may be a valid issue regarding something that is taking place at the other parent's house. In this case, we would want to have a mandated mental health professional in place that has a long-term relationship with our child. By law, this professional has to report to social services (CPS) anything that they think may be an issue regarding the safety of the child.

If your child tells you about their life with the other parent, or about other aspects of their life that are troublesome to you, tell them that you will make an appointment for them with their counselor so they can share what's going on. Professional counselors are mandated to make reports to child welfare agencies in certain situations. As impartial sources of information, the counselor will automatically have much more credibility than you will. If, on the other hand, the matter is of pressing concern and requires immediate attention, take your child directly to a children's hospital or to the family doctor to be examined and cared for.

Joey's Story

Katie had been divorced for four years, and had been dating the same man for the last two years. Six year old Joey had been diagnosed with ADD and was seeing a therapist. His parents both hoped that he could be helped without having to be put on medication. During his therapy sessions Joey often talked about how uncomfortable he was around Mom's boyfriend, Steve, even though he appeared to be a very nice guy who interacted easily and appropriately with Joey and his four year old brother, David. When Joey and his brother were together with their mom and her boyfriend, Katie noticed that Joey's agitation and his ADD seemed to be pronounced. She was truly concerned.

Joey's father, Tom, would constantly criticize Katie for her behavior and tell her that he completely disapproved of her relationship with her boyfriend. When he got worked up, which he often did during their communications, he would lay a number of other judgments on her as well.

Every time that Tom was with his son Joey, he would ask him what his mother was doing and about her relationship with Steve. When Joey asked Dad why he and Mom weren't together anymore, Tom always said it was because his mother was such a bad housekeeper. Joey started parroting this line to his mom.

After seeing Joey for a little over a month, it became clear to the therapist that Joey was making up stories for the benefit of each parent. He would tell Mom that Dad never helped him with his homework, and he would tell Dad that Mom was never around and that she was always with her boyfriend. The therapist recognized that Joey was telling each parent what he thought they wanted to hear. The child was extremely anxious all the time because he was carrying this terrific burden of trying to figure out what would make his parents happy and help them feel better. His diagnosis of ADD was nothing more than a medical assessment of his behaviors that were an acting-out of his anxieties.

In one therapy session that his father attended with him, Joey said that he knew his father was sad when he was alone and he knew this because he felt sad when he was alone. Later in that session the therapist made the recommendation to Tom that he begin to use the Mom's house/Dad's house portion of the parallel parenting model. She explained the process clearly to him and he point-blank refused to try it. His response was that in order to be a responsible parent he needed to know what was going on in his ex-wife's house "in order to teach the children right from wrong, which she clearly was not doing."

The therapist told him that he was making the adjustment to the divorce much harder for his children by constantly telling them what a bad person their mother was. The therapist also made it clear to him that the message he was sending the children was that they were responsible for making him happy, and that the only way they could do that was by telling him what he wanted to hear. She also shared with him that he was putting Joey between a rock and a hard place because he, Dad, always made a special point of grilling Joey about what happened at Mom's house. The therapist underlined her explanation to Tom by saying that Joey's ADD was nothing more than his way of dealing with the incredible stress he was experiencing in trying to take care of the feelings of both of his parents – an impossible task for anyone, let alone a six year old.

When the therapist presented the parallel parenting model to Katie, she immediately saw the wisdom of it and made a commitment to use it. She was so concerned about Joey and his younger brother that she was willing to learn how to work with her children in this new way, even though she was angry with Tom for his unrelenting badgering of their children.

Within a few weeks, Joey began to settle down when he was with his mother. With the passage of a few more weeks Joey began to relax when he was around Mom's boyfriend, Steve. Katie made it clear to Joey that he did not have to tell her anything about what went on at Dad's house, and that if anything came up that really bothered him he could feel free to share it with the therapist, whom he had come to really trust and feel safe with. Both Joey and Mom became more and more relaxed around each other, and his happy, easy-going nature started to shine through again.

Eventually, a pattern emerged. Whenever Joey returned to Mom's house from Dad's he was anxious and obviously stressed, but each time he would begin to relax a little sooner than the time before. It was clear that being at Mom's house had become a safe haven for him.

Separate Homes, Separate Rules, Separate Philosophies

Our rules, routines and philosophies are the glue that creates the stability in our children's lives. When they are at our house they should know exactly what to expect and what the consequences are. This clarity is critical in children's ability to feel safety and love. They know we love them because we set rules that keep them from being hurt. They may not like our rules right now, but in the long run they will most likely appreciate them.

In many high conflict cases one of the parents has little or no predictable structure in their lives. The parent is dependent on the child and there is noticeable chaos. It is essential that the children have structure in order to develop a sense of self and to be able to self-regulate. As their parent, we have to learn what is needed for that structure and provide it in a stable nurturing atmosphere.

Let Go of What Happens in the Other Parent's House

If we try to control what happens at the other parent's house, we only recreate the conflict from which we are trying so hard to distance ourselves. All we have the ability to do is to parent in a way that has a positive effect on our children in our own home. This is done through modeling our beliefs about right and wrong, and imparting our philosophies about the world to our children.

Children learn by what they see and experience. If the other parent's beliefs and philosophies are different, we need to have faith that our children will be able to figure out for themselves, in time, what is right and what works for them. If we don't do this we are selling our children short and we will greatly impair their self-esteem.

Children are smarter than we give them credit for. We need to trust that they can see that what we do "works" and that we have their best interests at heart. We need to keep our own house "clean" so that there is no basis for the accusations when they come.

Let Go of What the Other Parent is Saying to Your Child

Sometimes a parent attempts to get the children to choose between one parent or the other. This behavior ranges from subtle and unintentional to overt and on purpose. If this is true in your case, know that **it is what you do, rather than what you say, to your children that is critically important.**

Children have a great capacity to reason and to zero in on what is really going on. If what the other parent says is incongruent with the child's experience, the child will most likely figure that out. So if the child comes to you and says "Dad says you don't love me because you don't take me to the playground," rather than bashing Dad for what he said in front of the child, you can ask your child what s/he thinks. This response from you invites the child to trust their own experience of you. It is a confidence builder for them, and it disengages them from the emotionally draining experience of being stuck between their two parents. If you have a connected relationship with the child their answer will no doubt be something like this: "I know you love me because we do lots of things together." Let your child's response demonstrate what is true and what is not true regarding your relationship and the strength of your connection with them.

There's a second aspect to this scenario that we need to address. In all likelihood, if our former partner exhibits the kind of negative, blaming, finger-pointing behavior we saw in the example above, we cannot stop them from behaving like that. In fact, we will only make ourselves miserable trying to stop them. Any energy we put to defending or fighting this behavior will add fuel to the fire and is guaranteed to come back and burn us, as well as continuing the conflict. Instead of trying to change the other person, let's keep our focus on our relationship with our child.

Stay Out of the Other Parent's House

Here we introduce proven techniques for keeping the other parent out of our house and out of our thoughts. In order to accomplish this task, the reciprocal must also apply; as we focus on keeping the other parent out of our ongoing family life, we must also keep ourselves out of theirs.

Do not tell your children what you think of the other parent and do not judge your ex in front of the children. Better yet, don't judge them at all. By doing this you will spend less and less of your precious time thinking about the other parent and increase the distance and level of disengagement you are seeking. Let your children have whatever experience and relationship with the other parent that they are going to have. Let them judge for themselves and come to their own conclusions. Stay out of the middle of any conflicts or fights they may have with the other parent. Give them a counselor or mentor to talk to so they can be guided through what is going on for them, or encourage them to figure it out for themselves if they are capable of doing so.

A word to the wise: because we're human it is inevitable that our biases will come into play when we try to guide our children in matters that relate to the other parent. So don't try to "fix" that relationship, let the children work it out. If we try to work it out for them, it usually leads to contact and engagement—and the next thing we know, we're drawn back into the conflict.

"You cannot escape the responsibility of
tomorrow by evading it today."

-- Abraham Lincoln
(16th President of the United States, 1809-1865)

Chapter 8

Creating a Parenting Plan

One of the key characteristics of a strong parenting plan is that it will incorporate provisions for as little contact as possible between the parents. In addition, the parenting plan needs to include the following items:

Setting Boundaries around Communication

Avoid face-to-face exchanges: Here's why: when there is

more than one pick-up or drop-off during a week, parents will be in the "High Activation Cycle" (Chapter 5) most of the time, with the children along for the emotional ride. Every face-to-face exchange increases the potential for further conflict to develop.

No telephone conversations: No verbal contact except during rare emergencies! Experts suggest no verbal contact for the same reasons that face-to-face contact is not advisable. Each time the other parent's voice is heard, their face is imagined and stress levels shoot up. Verbal contact with the other parent leads to the possibility of an argument, an insult or manipulative behavior. Additionally, no one is keeping track of or documenting the conversation, so after-the-fact memories that eventually come forward are almost always inaccurate, and are the fuel that drives the battle of "he said/she said," inevitably landing us in our attorney's office again!

Email only: Communication is made only through email and other non-verbal and non-personal means, such as text messages, fax, or a neutral third party. Communication is made only when there is important information to be relayed (see *Important Information*, next page). Contents should include facts only. Keep personal opinions, sarcasm, and emotions out of the communication. Often one or both of the parents will try to draw the other into a fight through email. When this occurs, the parent who is being drawn into the fight may want to have someone else read the emails and pass along whatever requires a response. By having someone else read the email and act as the go-between, passing on only the required information, the parent will avoid the over stimulation that comes with reading the negative commentary from the other parent. Over time, this will stop the offending parent's behavior.

Better than email only: These days email isn't the most secure means of communication. In fact, I hear more and more from clients that the other parent has hacked their email and made changes to the contents. The best way to avoid this is to use one of the many online parenting programs now available. I recommend Our Family Wizard (www.ourfamilywizard.com). This program allows parents to virtually handle all of the business of parenting and stay disengaged from one another. It has a calendar for keeping track of the children's activities, a communication tool that replaces email and is secure from all potential tampering, a tool for keeping the accounting between the parents up to date, and much more. Courts around the country are ordering programs such as this because they can obtain the passwords and keep track of conversations between high conflict couples. This gives them valuable information and insight into which parent is perpetuating the conflict.

If the other parent doesn't want to communicate via email or one of the online programs, set a boundary. Simply state that if they wish to get a response, email is the only medium by which you will respond. We get to choose how we communicate and how much we disengage. This can be liberating and empowering as long as we hold the boundary.

By putting your communication in writing, you will have time to gather your thoughts and make sure that the tone is not argumentative. This also lets the receiving parent take some time to gather their thoughts so that they are less likely to blurt out an impulsive or angry response. Here are further essential guidelines for you. Each one is significant.

- Sarcasm is never helpful when trying to disengage from conflicts.
- Do not share your e-mails and faxes with your children. It is completely inappropriate for them to be privy to those communications, and/or used as a sounding board or witness for your communications.
- Try to limit non-emergency communication to twice a month, except for sharing information that is time sensitive (such as faxing a notice from school to the other parent on the day you receive it). Obviously, emergency information about

illnesses and injuries, unforeseen delays in visitation (as a result of traffic conditions, for example), and immediate school concerns should be shared by phone or text messaging, as soon as possible. However, by reducing general communication, and by putting all necessary communications in writing, you will go a long way towards disengaging from conflict.

Important information means only information that is about the health, welfare, and interests of your child. Examples: If your child is sick, you will inform the other parent of this fact, with details on what medication is needed, what has already been administered, and when the next dose is to be given. If your child has a school field trip, you will inform the other parent of the details and use your parenting plan to decide who might go with the child on the field trip. If you are the parent who receives your child's report card, copy it and send it to the other parent. Do this also with medical and extracurricular activity information, such as your child's little league schedule, as an example.

Develop relationships with your child's support systems

Each parent should develop independent relationships with their child's teachers, doctors, coaches, and friends so that they don't have to rely on the other parent for information. For example, be sure to take turns taking your child to the doctor and dentist so that you have firsthand knowledge of what is going on. Instead of seeing these trips as burdens, see them as positive indicators of your independence.

Planning vs. Complaining

Do not complain to the other parent when s/he is ten minutes late for an exchange of your child, and don't argue over whose turn it is to be responsible for your child's next haircut. Simply put, get out of the business of doing battle with your ex! Have parameters in your parenting plan for these kinds of situations so that you are prepared, and don't let your feathers get ruffled. To put it another way, take care of your children's needs as if the other parent didn't exist.

Many of the parents I work with have a huge problem with the concept of what is and what isn't fair. They lose track of the damage they are inflicting on the children by maintaining a position that has little or no importance in the big picture. The loss of a day here and there until you can get the parenting plan in order isn't worth continuing the conflict at the cost of the children's wellbeing.

Support yourself by being prepared with systems that foster the freedom that you deserve as a parent. When other odd or unusual situations crop up that have not been dealt with in your plan, do your best to let them play themselves out whenever they are not essential. By "play themselves out, I mean don't react to the situation; rather, create a solution so it doesn't occur again. Remember that the less emotional charge you have, the smoother things will be.

The Essential Details of a Strong Parenting Plan

Your parenting plan is the piece of the puzzle that is going to insulate you from most of the causes of the conflict. It needs to be detailed; as detailed as possible so there's no room for argument. You should keep a conformed (court stamped) copy of the parenting plan with you both at home and in your car. Your parenting plan must include specifics of the day of the week and time of the day for pick up and drop off, for example. Be specific – not just "after school". If kids are not always in school, establish a time and place for the exchange. This includes three-day weekends, school furlough days, school breaks and summertime or vacation time, among other things. Everything needs to be absolutely specified so if the police or other authorities show up, you can say, "It's all right here."

Preferably, child pick up and drop off should be at school, daycare or a neutral third party site. It should specify who is allowed to pick up the kids from school, or from any other activity that they're involved in.

Holiday schedules need to be specific about when the holiday starts and ends. For example, does Thanksgiving start when they get out of school on Wednesday and end on Sunday night or Monday morning? Do you get four days, or only Thanksgiving Day? And if it means Thanksgiving Day, does that mean from 8:00 a.m. to 6:00 p.m., or from Wednesday night to Thursday night or from Thursday morning to Friday morning? Again, what time? The message here is that you need to be specific. Some of the biggest outbursts I've seen in high conflict custody situations are due to the lack of this type of detail.

A day here, a day there; interpretation of the parenting plan that one parent thinks is one way and the other parent thinks is another leads to this suggestion: If there's something you fought over in the past, get a mediator. Get somebody to sit down and figure it out. Write it in. If your parenting plan is already in place, make an amendment. Change the parenting plan so you don't encounter the problem again. If you faced it once, you're most likely going to face it again.

If a parent goes on an extended vacation, and has two (separate) weeks with the children each year, decide ahead of time whether they can take their two vacation weeks with the children consecutively. If possible, have a plan in place to balance the equation. Again, this should be part of the parenting plan. Write provisions for trading weeks in case there is a family emergency. Then, clearly define what a family emergency is. To me, it's very limited. It's a death or severe accident in the family; it's a wedding in the family – those are emergencies, and are things your children need an opportunity to be a part of, as it will impact their entire lives. This includes events that are a big deal or once-in-a-lifetime opportunities, or something that can't be rearranged. Say, for example, that Grandma just gave them tickets for a trip to Paris, Barcelona and Greece. Here's an opportunity for them to see the world and it's during your week. Are you going to stop them from going? I sure hope not, but many parents in high conflict divorce and custody disputes will do just that.

These events benefit the child, and that's what this should be about. Opportunities for them to enrich their lives; and you don't have to get a week back because you let them go. You might say, "That's what my ex always does and it's just not fair." What isn't fair is that your children think there is even a possibility that they can't go on such a trip or to an important family event.

You have a choice. You can allow these types of events to happen easily and you can do it without asking for anything in return. In the end, it's a lot easier on everybody—especially your children. You don't have to rearrange a schedule. Your kids can live a week without you. It's not the end of the world. They're going to be in your life forever. You might actually find that you get a little bit of breathing room and may even remember what silence sounds like. You can recharge and go have some fun (and that's important as well). Many times, parents spend too much time focusing on, "I have to have the same amount of time as the other parent. I have to have my piece. I have to have my fair share, my time." This is a distorted way of thinking.

A strong parenting plan includes specific material that sets and helps maintain good boundaries. Every parenting plan should include the following:

- Provisions for phone contact with the children. If you think about it for very long you will agree that phone contact with your children is more for you than for them. Further, there is a good chance that the other parent will make excuses for them to not talk to you or even flatly deny the call. In either case the likelihood of getting the court to be effective in the solution is low. Believe it or not, less is more.

- Day(s) of the week and time(s) of day for pick-up and drop-off of the children.
- Place for child pick-up and drop-off (preferably at school or day care, or some other neutral site).
- Persons who are allowed to pick up the children.
- Holiday schedules with specifics about when the holiday starts and ends.
- Summer schedule, if different from school schedule.
- Vacation schedule (how many weeks and if they can be concurrent): If a parent goes on an extended vacation each year and has two weeks with the children each year, pre-decide whether they can take their two vacation weeks with the children consecutively.
- Provisions for trading weeks in case of a family emergency. Define what constitutes "an emergency."
- Provisions for deaths or severe accidents, weddings or birthdays. These are events that your children must have an opportunity to be a part of. Family celebrations are a big deal. Things that will happen only once in a lifetime and cannot be rearranged.

Ultimately, the parenting plan becomes the court order for custody and visitation. By including these items in the parenting plan you are further creating structure for the boundaries essential for parallel parenting and stopping the high conflict cycle. Once you get your parenting plan established, no changes. You make no changes and you don't ask any favors of that parenting plan. Unless it falls into one of the categories mentioned, you don't give any, either. **If you start to make exceptions to the plan, the**

plan goes to junk and the boundaries are lost. This is your boundary. This is how you get to establish the distance from the other parent that you need. No changes for two years.

Why two years? It takes about that long for the conflict to have an opportunity to really come to rest. After two years, you might find that you're not as angry at the end of those two years, that you're done fighting about the silverware, you're done fighting about the custody, and you're done fighting about whatever it is that you were fighting about.

Your focus has been on your children so much that now you may find you can try to co-parent. This is the best possible outcome. You can put your toe in the pond and see if the water is okay. And if it is, you go in a little bit further. If it's still okay, you go in a little bit further and you start to try to co-parent. If you see the alligators on the other shore start to scramble for the water, get out and go back to the parenting plan.

What Happens if the Other Parent Breaks a Court Order

The first step is to assess the intent behind the disruption of the order:

- Was it a simple act of defiance or was it an unavoidable occurrence?
- Was this the first time or has there been a string of similar occurrences?
- Is there something that can be put into place so it doesn't happen again (such as an addendum to the parenting plan)?

The next thing to do is assess the risk-to-reward for starting any legal action or even having an attorney write a letter. There are several key questions that need to be asked:

- Am I going to spend more money to rectify the problem than I will get back, either monetarily or in another benefit such as emotional freedom?
- How will it disrupt my family?
- What will the overall impact be in boundary setting vs. creating further conflict?

After making these assessments you then decide what your proper course of action should be. **Court and attorneys should be the last place you seek recourse unless the infraction is egregious.** It is a good idea to put a clause in the divorce agreement naming a mediator who is retained to solve problems that might arise in the future if they cannot be easily resolved by the two parents.

The rules of the parenting plan are broken all the time. Oftentimes, the court's response is to do little, if anything—often it's just a token slap on the wrist. Again, be sure to assess what is really important here. What can you really change? What outcome would be worth the time/energy/money expenditure required to achieve it? Is this something to log for future use, perhaps in a larger family court issue down the road?

"I look to the future because that's where I am going to spend the rest of my life."

-- George F. Burns
(American comedian, 1896 - 1996)

Chapter 9

Connecting With Your Children

When parents divorce they often discover that they need to find new ways to connect with their children. The family structure has changed dramatically and the present family is looking for ways to reconnect and adapt. It is critical to understand the feelings and anxieties that can come up for children at this time.

Often, children are driven by the fear of what could happen next that will further destabilize their world. They are left off-balance—unsure if their parents are even going to stay in their lives. At this time it is essential for us to be available to them—to be present and child-focused when we are with them, and to keep connecting in ways both large and small.

One way of connecting with the children is through family activity and the processes associated with planning these activities. I do not mean taking the kids to Disneyland or some amusement park. These places are a distraction and don't bring you together with your children. What I do mean is to plan activities that demand your total presence with your children. Time in nature, hiking, swimming, cooking; where the attention is on both you and the children, and not on some over-stimulating distraction. Here are a couple of examples that show both sides of what to do vs. what not to do.

A parent in one of my classes shared that she would often take her child to Chucky Cheese and would be there with the child watching her play. Another parent in the same class would take their child to the park playground, and get in the tunnels and slides and engage with his son, chasing him and following his lead. Can you see the difference in the quality of time that was spent? Which child do you think will remember their time ___with their parent?___

Genuine Expectation Opportunities (GEOs)

When you plan activities with your children, for the near future and well into the future, you instill into the child's mind the understanding that you will be with them always; that you are their rock. The steps you take to prepare for these activities, like looking at pictures and maps, or shopping for supplies for the activities, will keep you in their consciousness all the time. I call this creating "Genuine Expectation Opportunities" or GEOs. When there is always a family activity in the planning stages children feel deeply reassured. For them, making plans into the future translates into "we will always be together. Having activities on the calendar to look forward to, and being actively engaged in an ongoing planning process when they are with you, will keep the children connected to a place they feel safe, especially if the other parent's house is not a place where they feel safe or connected.

By using GEOs you are teaching your children skills that they will need in their adult lives, such as planning, budgeting, self-discipline and leadership, as well as goal setting and completion for things that they want. One of the great things about planning short, medium, and long-term family activities is that the activities can be built around available financial resources, for example, and really don't need to cost much. Furthermore, creating a plan and budget for these activities can be one of the most important and valuable aspects of this process.

Find out what kinds of things the children are interested in. Each member will have different interests so, over time, each person in the family gets to choose what the activity is to be. That person takes a leadership role and the rest of the family offers support. Even young children need to have leadership roles.

Creating a schedule of activities that extends into the future—each with a different "leader"—will ensure that each child, no matter their age, gets to have their say. This will teach them that their needs and ways of having fun are recognized. You will be amazed at the benefit your family will realize by taking this approach. The youngest children will probably surprise you with their leadership abilities, and the older ones will have a fabulous opportunity to discover how nurturing they can be <u>and</u> how much they enjoy being the nurturers. To think that all of these learning experiences can take place under the category of "Having Fun"!

Parents often complain that their children either don't want to talk about what they would like to do for "fun", or don't know how to figure it out. I tell them that, especially in the beginning, it can take time for the children to adjust to the notion of their family having fun together for a change! If parents are willing to be patient, the continued discussion about ways to have fun together will begin to draw the children out. Frequently children are reticent when they are with the parent who was not their primary caregiver. Just remember that it takes time to create a new relationship with the children and for them to feel comfortable with the new family arrangement.

Mike's Story

Mike was a client who had recently divorced. He hadn't had much of a relationship with his two teenaged girls and suddenly found himself having to deal with parenting them by himself half the time. Mike had poor communication skills when it came to his daughters, and the older one (age 15) was extremely angry over the divorce. During the time he was attending my 12-week High Conflict Diversion Program™, Mike was skeptical about our strategies to help parents connect with their children. He tried to enter into dialog with his daughters, offering a number of suggestions about possible future events they could do together as a family. He got little response.

Part of the problem was that Mike was making all of the suggestions and not inviting the girls to participate in the process of imagining what would be fun for them to do together. Eventually, they did make a few tentative suggestions, but overall there was still little feedback from his daughters. We encouraged him to stay positive and to keep trying to elicit their input.

At our normal check-in on Mike's last night of class (when each parent has to talk about something that happened during the week that brought them joy), Mike told the story of how his older daughter had come to him and shared that she had found his old scuba diving log. She said to her father, "Dad, do you remember how, when I was 10 years old, you kept telling me that you would take me to get my diving certification when I was 14? Well, that is what I want us to do as a family." It turned out that both daughters agreed that that was what they wanted to do.

Mike was smiling from ear to ear in class because they'd finally identified the activity they had been looking for! He also shared how excited he was about the possibilities for family discussion that would be taking place as they made their plans to get the girls licensed and head out on their first scuba dive. He knew they'd hit the jackpot with a real way to connect and explore their new relationships as a family. He realized that the possibilities for family fun were virtually endless. Often, it can take awhile for the children to jump in with enthusiasm. Patience and commitment to the process on your part are essential. The rewards are well worth it, guaranteed!

Create a Timeline of Events and Activities

Family time in our lives is an important touchstone in creating happy memories of our childhood, as well as helping us feel we are an important part of our family. Memories of connected time spent with our parents are part of what we hold onto when things get hard later in life. This is the foundation that gives us the ability to feel our connection and importance when life gets difficult.

Find Out What Interests Your Children

Parents often plan activities for the family without taking the wants and needs of the children into consideration. How often have you planned a trip or outing and had the children rebel against the idea? Children are being told what is going to happen and when it's going to happen all the time. This is not empowering to them nor does it create any life skills. Children need to have input and decision-making power in the family. If they don't learn it here, how are they going to be empowered in their adult life to know how to make decisions? We certainly don't want other people making all their decisions for them, do we?

Short-term activities are scheduled one to three weeks out and can be as simple as planning a special family meal or a family activity at home (e.g., Monopoly night, movie night, a picnic at the park or a camping trip in the backyard). There are infinite possibilities: just get in and explore them with your kids! Each event has a designated leader. The leader gets to do the planning, set the budget and work with the rest of the family to delegate other activities that go into the event. This can become a monthly activity that rotates leadership—a different family member is the leader each month.

Another example of a short-term activity would be a planned day trip with a focus on nature: hiking, going to tide pools, rock collecting, fishing, etc. Whatever the activity, make sure that planning and budgeting are an integral part of the process that leads up to the activity. (Family bonding occurs as much in the planning phase as in the activity itself.) There is something wonderful that happens when the activities take place in nature—all the senses are involved and time has a wonderful way of stopping as you become immersed in and get to really appreciate the beauty all around you. Family activities in nature provide some of the most lasting memories that can be reawakened by a simple smell, sound, sight or touch.

Medium-term activities are scheduled three to six months out, and these can have a larger impact on the imaginations of the children because there is more lead time to create "positive anticipation." An example of a medium-term activity would be a weekend camping trip. Nature is a perfect backdrop for family bonding in such activities because they involve all of the senses and thus have a greater impact on the memory of the children. Start the planning process by asking the children where they would like to go and what they would like to do. Turn this into a win-win opportunity by asking for their input from the beginning.

Once you have decided on your destination, take out maps, look on the Internet together, and begin an outline of your plans. Be sure that even the smallest details are included in the list of things you will need to do and prepare. This degree of detail will reward you immensely in the end. Be sure that you and your children look at the plan together at least twice a week—refine it and add to it as the excitement builds. Make sure that each and every family member has a role to play that will be appropriately challenging and rewarding for them.

Plan a budget for the entire trip and discuss the children's roles in saving for it. Give them opportunities to make/save money for the things they may want to do on the trip so they don't have to ask you for money when you get there. For a child, there is nothing like having their own money and being able to choose how they spend it. This approach is another fabulous opportunity for building self-worth and helping your children feel a sense of accomplishment.

Long-term activities can be built on the medium-term activities or they can stand alone. These activities are planned six months to one year out and have all of the same aspects of the medium-term activities. This might be the family vacation or some other special group activity.

A great way to keep track of what is to come is by creating a vision board. This helps make the activity real and generate enthusiasm. As a family, sit down with a sheet of poster board, magazines, glue and scissors and launch into creating a group collage of the outing you envision. Cut out pictures and slogans that capture the essence and details of your weekend outing. By establishing these ongoing activities and committing to the planning and bonding processes involved in them, you are instantly establishing a precious timeline for them to attach to during this period when their lives feel scattered and unstable.

As you plan and take part in these activities with your children you have the opportunity to find out what really excites them, what motivates them, and where their strengths lie. You are given the priceless opportunity to sit and listen to your children dream, discover their talents and abilities, and awaken to new experiences. The journey is what is important here, not the destination!

If you choose to fully engage in this GEO process you will be amazed at how quickly your relationship with your children grows, and how the level of communication between you is enhanced. Further, you will find that your children begin to talk to you more freely and in a trusting manner about the things in their world.

Now, sit down with the family and begin to brainstorm your family Genuine Expectation Opportunities (GEOs).

1. Start by making a list of the activities that pop up as you do your GEO brainstorming. This is really the time to give yourself the opportunity to make a fresh start and to dream together as a family. Take advantage of this opportunity to come up with new ways to have fun together, as well as to do things that your children have been wanting to do while you've been otherwise engaged in the conflict. Suggestions: (a) have one of your children be the scribe for this list; (b) spend enough time doing this so that everyone is engaged, but be sure you move on to the next step while the energy is still high!

2. Now you can all dive into the early planning phase. Start a second list that's got three blank pages. (Make another child the scribe.) From the activities you all brainstormed, pick one that would be a short-term GEO, one that would be a medium-term GEO, and one that would be a long-term GEO activity. Write the name of each activity at the top of one of the blank pages. (Be prepared: there may be some lively discussion on the way to pick the activities that end up on this list! Notice which activities get a strong vote of approval and which don't. This is valuable information! Also, remind everyone that nothing is set in stone at this point. Your goal right now is to launch

yourselves into the adventure of dreaming, brainstorming and planning as a family.)

Continuing to brainstorm, begin each list with the specific things that will need to be done for that activity to happen. Plan in detail! If a child shows particular interest in contributing to or taking responsibility for a particular step, write her/his name down next to that item. After you've been at this for a time but while the energy is still high, move on to Step 3. You'll have plenty of opportunity to continue to work on these three pages of planning notes over the next weeks and months until each activity HAPPENS!

3. (a) Now create your three Master GEO lists for short-term, medium-term, and long-term activities. Look again at the activities you brainstormed originally in Step 1. Write each one on one of your Master Lists. These lists are going to be your ongoing reference lists, to be added to and amended as you go along.
   (b) Set a date for creating your family vision boards for each one of your GEOs.

NOTE: Be sure that you keep all these lists in a safe place (a folder in a file cabinet, for example) because you'll want to refer to them over and over again.

"I have always argued that change becomes stressful and overwhelming only when you've lost any sense of the constancy of your life. You need firm ground to stand on. From there, you can deal with that change."

-- Richard Nelson Bolles
(Author, *What Color is Your Parachute?*, 1927 -   )

Chapter 10

Transitions & Traditions

If one of the parents is remarried there may be blended families to deal with, presenting the challenges of learning, accepting, and integrating different social behaviors, structures and cultures. Creating comfortable and dependable transitions can be a huge help in assisting the children's adjustment from one household to the other.

When children go from one set of rules and family dynamics to another they need consistent ways to transition—to reorient themselves to where they are now, who they are with and what the rules are here. The dynamics at Mom's house and Dad's house are most likely very different and require a stable way for them to move between the two environments.

As we read earlier about John and Kimberly, we know

that the children may arrive from the other parents' house behaving chaotically and out of control, have regressed. These behaviors are the child's way of coping with changes in their life, and in many cases have little or nothing to do with the other parent. By creating structured and dependable transitions for every time the children come and go from your house you are giving them time to adjust, consistency they can count on, and a new way to cope.

Preparing for the Drop-Off

You may feel anxious about letting the children go to the other parent, and they may feel anxious as well. Get everything ready the night before so there is no anxiety about not having things ready to go. Creating a transition ritual to bring your time together to an end can take the stress out of the adjustment for everyone. A visit to your Genuine Expectation Opportunities as discussed in the previous chapter can help connect the children back to the next time they will be with you and give them a sense of continuity in their lives. You may want to have an ongoing puzzle set up somewhere in the house that you spend time working on before they leave and again when they come home (Lego's work well, too). This kind of dependable and quieting activity can help ease the children through their transition every time they shuttle between their two homes. It can help them "complete the circle" by bridging them from one environment to the other and back again.

Another factor in children's anxiety about the transition comes from their concern about the parent they're leaving. Be sure that you have fun things planned for yourself during the time your children are with the other parent so that your children don't think you are going to be lost without them. Let them know you are going to have plenty to do in their absence and that you're already looking forward to having them back at home with you. (Reassuring them of this can be more important than you realize!)

Children need time to transition between one house and the next. School or daycare can serve as a helpful part of the transition; however, adding an activity through which they can specifically connect with you can be extremely helpful. It doesn't have to be fussy or fancy; even something as simple as stopping to get a soda or snack can serve as a powerful transition tool. This casual stop in neutral territory can provide precious decompression time for your children, as well as a light, easy-going time of reconnection for all of you.

When the Children Come Home

Often the children are wired and anxious when they return home, depending on their stay with the other parent and the degree of continuing conflict that they have been subjected to. Taking time to stop and connect with them before you get home is important. Shopping for some of the items for the GEOs can help all of you pick up where you left off when you were dreaming of and planning for your family activities. Going to a fun place for a treat (such as McDonalds or Baskin-Robbins) can be a great transition as well. What a bonus, too, to have your loving and caring contact become associated with the tastes and smells that your children enjoy.

Physical activity can help defray some of the nervous energy that might have built up. You'll feel more relaxed afterwards and that will make it easier for all of you to settle in together at home. This is another great way for all of you to transition.

Use your imagination and discuss with your children what transition rituals might work for all of you. It could be taking the dog for a walk, a trip to the park, a special hike, feeding the ducks at the local pond, a trip to the market to buy ingredients for everyone's favorite meal, or making sure that everyone is involved in helping prepare dinner on their first night back; anything you and your children agree on is an option. As surprising as it may sound, simply discussing these transition activities and asking for each child's opinion can prove to be a great way to connect with your children. The most important thing here is that you choose one and only one and do that activity every time they transition. The children will find it to be stabilizing and calming.

Here's an example of how a mom helped her child deal with the transitions between parents and homes:

Wendy was having trouble with the transition of her 3-year-old daughter, Sofia, to and from the other parent's house. Sofia would get clingy prior to going to her father's and would make a fuss about not wanting to go. During one of our classes we asked Wendy where the pick-ups and drop-offs were taking place. She told us they were happening at a local strip mall parking lot. After we learned that one of the stores in the mall was a pet store, we counseled Wendy to use the pet store for Sofia's transition ritual.

Thereafter, every time there was a transition to the father's house, Wendy would take Sofia to the pet store 20 minutes prior to the father's arrival. They would pet the bunnies and kittens and check out the new puppies. The contact with the animals was soothing to Sofia and by the time Dad arrived she was ready to go with no problems.

Wendy also created a ritual for Sofia's reverse transition time. When she met Sofia for pick-up they would stop to get a bagel and hot chocolate before going home. This was time Sofia had to talk to mom before they entered into their routine at Wendy's house. It turned out to be a really special time between the two of them that each really looked forward to.

Traditions

After you have separated from the other parent, all of

the traditional activities become difficult, at best. If you go about trying to do the same things that you used to do at the same times and in the same ways there is always going to be the sense that someone is missing. It is confusing and often disturbing to the children. Going on the same vacations, doing the same things over the holidays and for birthdays can become uncomfortable. Therefore, creating new family traditions is vitally important. Some of the ways traditions help settle the family into a more stable and safe unit are by creating events that are predictable, comfortable and reassuring. They give us a break from having to "make up" our lives every minute.

Regardless of our age, traditions can have a profound effect upon us. Although traditions are commonly thought of as social conventions that are adopted by large segments of our society (like Christmas trees or flag-flying on the 4th of July), precious traditions that are fondly remembered can also be created by each family.

Traditions can be simple or they can be amazingly complex. What is important is that they be easy, dependable and something everyone looks forward to. One example might be rotating each year which child in the family lights the first Hanukkah candle. Then that child gets to pick which game the group will play that evening.

As we know, when the family breaks up, all that is normal and stable goes out the window. The children are left in a state of confusion and shock. It is essential to create new touchstones of stability. Creating new traditions is a perfect way to bring stability to the new family unit.

Building Family Unity

Traditions should include activities for all members of the family, no matter how young or old. They should be occasions when the entire family comes together— at the same time every day, week, month, or year—occasions that can be counted on and looked forward to. Traditions teach us to take care of each other by participating together in the activity and helping one another to prepare and complete the event. Traditions honor the past and embrace the future.

Out with the Old, In with the New

Birthdays

Because of the actual dates of child-sharing in the parenting plan, celebrating a birthday or holiday on the actual day may not be possible. Just remember that the celebration really can happen anytime before or after the actual date. In fact, families often change the date of a special occasion to make it easier for more people to attend a party. Trying to make sure the children are with a particular parent on that parent's birthday or a holiday can create situations that cause conflict to arise once again. Do your best to work with your children to create alternate dates and other ways to celebrate special occasions. (Celebrating a birthday two times can be twice as much fun as celebrating just once!). Create traditions with the kids that include the participation of everyone in the family, such as serving them breakfast in bed, decorating their room before they come home from school or work, or planning a celebration of any kind. This tradition gets repeated every year for everyone in the family.

Holidays: A New Perspective

You have the opportunity to get creative here! All you are trying to achieve is the continuity that the children need. There's no reason that occasions have to be celebrated the way they were before. Instead of falling into (or staying stuck in) a rut as to how you celebrate a particular holiday, take advantage of the opportunity to do a little stretching yourself. If you "don't bake," bake cookies with your children. If you "don't think of Mexican food as holiday food," make Mexican food a part of your new tradition!

GEOs can be a part of the new traditions. I have clients that have an annual camping trip to the same place with friends and family; another that goes with his son to see a different NFL stadium every year in the summer—this GEO will take them well into the child's adulthood. That is precisely what I want you to create: traditions that your children will potentially pass along to their children.

Ideas for New Traditions

Sit down with your children and brainstorm three new family traditions. Consider coming up with them in different categories. Here are a few suggestions to get you started:

Birthdays: Decorate the outside of the birthday person's bedroom door before they wake up the morning of their birthday; create a special birthday plate and/or hat that the celebrant gets to use that whole day; have each member of the family make a birthday card for the birthday boy or girl and sharing what they love about that person. (Be sure to make these cards the week before—this creates excitement and positive anticipation!)

Vacations: Playing a particular game or singing a special goofy song in the car as you head off on vacation; making wearable mini-scrapbooks of the best pictures from your summer vacation using iron-on transfers on T-shirts; planning and doing one craft project together every month of summer vacation. For ideas go to a craft store or check out the internet for cool websites.

Visit to Grandparents: "Show and Tell": Each family member brings something they've been working on (such as a craft, a trading card collection, an art work). Or, if the project isn't portable, s/he gets time to give a little "presentation," complete with photos to share about what s/he's been working on.

Holidays: Get into the spirit of the holiday by visiting an aging relative or an aging neighbor you haven't spent time with for awhile; make your own Hanukkah candles or your own Christmas tree ornaments labeled with name and year; read a holiday-appropriate story out loud ("The Night Before Christmas" on Dec. 24; the *Declaration of Independence* or "Preamble" to *The Constitution* on July 4 and lighting sparklers afterwards); collect food for a local homeless shelter on Thanksgiving; make a family resolution on New Year's Day (write it down, seal it and save it until the following New Year's Eve to open); serve an all-green meal on St. Patrick's Day.

"We do not believe in ourselves until someone reveals that deep inside us is valuable, worth listening to, worthy of our trust, sacred to our touch. Once we believe in ourselves we can risk curiosity, wonder, spontaneous delight or any experience that reveals the human spirit."

-- E.E. Cummings
(American poet, painter, essayist, playwright, 1894 - 1962)

Chapter 11

Self-Care & Rediscovery

Divorce, let alone high conflict divorce, is a time of great stress. It is a time of not knowing what to expect in so many aspects of life. Divorce can leave you in a state of exhaustion and depression, and feeling disconnected from the things that were once touchstones of normalcy. For many, this is a time when healthy self-care practices are abandoned, although they are needed now more than ever.

Ironically, it's especially during this time of high stress that you really have to be at your best. You can't afford to let the stress of the conflict prevent you from being fully present for the critical tasks that you are required to complete. The list is long, and it includes preparing for court, staying steady in your work environment, and staying fully present for your children.

This is not the time to let your attention to self-care slide! This is the time to go the extra mile to take care of yourself. True, when you first get out of a marriage or relationship you may feel like you have just been released from a cage. Yes, you probably feel like you need to break loose and have some fun. But be wary! This kind of behavior often leads to overindulgence in areas you're unaccustomed to overindulging in—food, drink, drugs or just playing too hard and not getting enough rest.

On the other hand, you may find that the stress of the situation doesn't leave you feeling like partying. You may find yourself unable to sleep, or your mind-chatter stuck in "worry" mode, preventing you from relaxing. Additionally, lack of sleep and negative mind-chatter can leave you in a state of depletion—at a time when the divorce challenges are changing at a rapid pace and the pressure to stay on top of everything is overwhelming. (And you have to take on all of the responsibilities of the other parent, as well!) Granted, you are likely to get breaks every week when the other parent has the children, but the time spent with the children may well be more intense as they process the changes in relationship, too.

When we aren't taking care of ourselves, we also won't be able to take care of our children properly, doubling the negative impact. There is also the question of what is being modeled for the children: is it loving self-care or its opposite?

You will see three lists on the following page: habits that contribute to the stress cycle, practices that counter the effects of stress, and side effects of protracted stress.

Habits that contribute to the stress cycle	Practices that counter the effects of stress	Side effects of protracted stress

• Drugs
• Alcohol
• Sugar and overeating
• Lethargy
• Withdrawal from social activity
	• Exercise
	• Meditation
	• Visualization
	• Nutrition
	  • *Supplementation*
	  • *Diet*
	• Social engagement
		• Memory is not as good
		• Diminished discernment around decision-making
		• Parent's energies are depleted with the children and in all other areas of life (work, personal relationships, court proceedings, etc.)
		• Overwhelm sets in
		• Increased illness
		• Decreased sense of satisfaction in life
		• Sleep disturbance
		• Increased anxiety
		• Weight loss/ weight gain
		• Poor concentration
		• Difficulty relaxing
		• Snapping at loved ones/ stressed personal relationships

Would you not agree that it's well worth it to replace the *Habits that contribute to the stress cycle* with the *Practices that counter the effects of stress* in order to avoid those nasty *Side effects of protracted stress*?

All of these side effects of poor self-care contribute to the high conflict cycle. Something to consider: all of these things are in your control. When you begin to manage them you are able to reduce the effects of the conflict and to enhance the resiliency you need to meet the special demands that manifest during this stressful time.

Overindulgence in drugs, alcohol, or other distractions will inhibit your ability to stay present and keep your thinking clear and sharp. Because of the potential long-term ramifications, the wrong move here, such as a DUI, will cost you dearly in your efforts to have substantial custody with your children. This just isn't the time to "let it all hang out."

On the contrary, it is very much the time to clearly assess your situation, consolidate your assets, and plan your future. That assessment needs to begin with an honest reevaluation of your past, done in a way that allows you to think clearly so you don't jump in and recreate the same scenarios that got you here. Your responsibility to yourself and your children requires this type of mature response on your part. This is a great time to be working with a good therapist.

At the same time, this isn't to say that breaking out and having some fun isn't important. Social interaction is, in fact, one of the most important aspects of self-care. Social contact is critical for humans because it gives us enjoyment and companionship, a source of acknowledgment of what we are going through, and a sense of being supported by other people who care. Simply choose your activities in a way that will support your efforts of positive self-care.

Time spent outside in nature with friends can and does bring great relief in times of stress. The word recreation means "to re-create," or to renew yourself. (If your recreation comes from overindulgence it doesn't serve this purpose and leaves your mind and body at a greater deficit.) Hike, swim, play, have fun with your friends and—above all—moderate the type of substances you put in your body that take a toll on your overall well-being.

Start Feeling Better

In the process of feeling better, I would like to

introduce the idea of another kind of indulgence: that of treating yourself to a regular routine of activities that have a positive impact on your well-being. Take time every week to get pampered; get a massage, a manicure, a facial or your hair done.

Consider scheduling regular "mental health days." This will help keep the stress from piling up. This self-care technique will leave you relaxed and feeling like you can take on anything. Once adopted, this practice could become an automatic, positive habit that will enhance the quality of your life for the rest of your life. If things are particularly stressful, take a "mental health day" (call the office and tell your boss you are calling in because you are *blind—you just can't see* coming to work today!).

You may not have the finances may not be there to do some of these things on a regular basis, but find some way to pamper yourself. Cook a special dinner for yourself, take a hot bubble bath, sunbath, etc.

The following exercise can help you relax anytime and anywhere:

Five simple little steps to freedom: This exercise will help clear your mind and settle your nervous system. If you take time to practice this when there is very little stress in your day; when there is a time of great stress, it will work quickly to change your brain chemistry and help calm you down.

1. Acknowledge the thoughts you have and how they make you feel. Put them in a box.
2. Begin taking long deep breaths. Imagine the breath is coming through your heart.
3. Give yourself the gift of a pleasant memory. This could be a person, place or experience that gives you joy to think about.
4. Allow all of your attention to be on your breath, your heart and your pleasant memory. If your mind wanders, gently bring it back. Stay with this for a minimum of two minutes. Once you feel relaxation set in, notice how your heart feels, and also any body sensations you are experiencing.
5. With your heart, ask what you can do with the things in the box.
6. Listen with your heart for the answer.

Rediscovering Your Identity

During the time you spend in relationship you can easily lose track of yourself, who you are, and what you believe. It is an all–too-common phenomenon for people to mold themselves into becoming someone they are not in order to preserve the peace. It is also a profoundly human belief that what you know is safer than what you don't know, especially in terms of change and how your relationship may be affected. The idea of changing a behavior pattern is intrinsically threatening and scary, but breaking your old patterns of behavior is essential to both changing the conflict dynamic and discovering your own power.

Time For Transformation

Used wisely, this can be a time of great transformation. Suddenly, you have an opportunity to explore the things you would like most to do with your future. There is an opportunity for self-inquiry that might not have been available when you were in a relationship. You have time to look at what went wrong in your former relationship, to assess what your responsibility was. You can create new ways of thinking that keep you from repeating those old patterns so that in your next relationship you have all of the tools for success and knowledge, as well as the personal resources not to lose yourself again.

Risk Taking

This can also be a time to test your risk-taking abilities—time to try things you have always wanted to try but were afraid to. We have a responsibility to our children to give them permission to test their world. If we don't model that for them, how can they trust that it is okay for them to take risks?

"Security is mostly a superstition. It does not exist in nature nor do children as a whole experience it. Avoiding danger is no safer in the long run than outright exposure. Life is either a daring adventure, or nothing.

"To keep our faces toward change and behave like free spirits in the presence of fate is strength undefeatable."

-- Helen Keller
American Author and Educator, *The Open Door,* 1880 - 1968)

The quotes above are two of my favorites. To me, these quotes speak to the essence of life—that all things are possible and that life is meant to be one spontaneous adventure. Unfortunately, as adults, we forget this so completely that we end up making the attainment of security our life's goal.

Take the quotes from Helen Keller, copy them and put them somewhere that you can see them frequently and make them something you begin to live your life by. You will likely find that by doing so every aspect of life becomes new and exciting.

EXERCISES:
Self-care

1. What are the areas of self-care that drop off for you? Make a column on a piece of paper and write down the areas in which you abandon self-care during the conflict.

2. In another column write down what effects occur from this lack of self-care.

3. In the last column, write down at least 5 things that could become (or already have become) a problem in

your divorce or custody case as a result of the side effects of poor self-care. Remember to include the costs your children are paying, as well. This will help you recognize more clearly the effects of poor self-care on you and your children.

Transition

1. What are some things you would like to try in your life? How does thinking about doing these things make you feel? Does it bring up excitement, fear, sadness, or something else?

2. Take some time to explore why those feeling may be coming up. Write down your thoughts.

4. Ask yourself:
   a. "What is stopping me from doing these things?"
   b. "What would I have to change in order to do them?"
   c. If the other parent were no longer a factor in your life, what things would you do differently?
   d. Is the other parent stopping you from doing these things? If so, how?

5. What are the qualities you feel you lost when you were in the relationship, and/or the dreams you gave up in the relationship (or when you became a parent). What was the belief that made you give up those qualities and dreams?

6. Ask yourself: "If I could return to those qualities and dreams, what would have to change in my thinking?" Now ask yourself: "Are any of those changes something that I would like to integrate into my new identity?"

   Exploring these questions may give you insights into

some of your core beliefs—about how you "should" or "shouldn't" live your life, what is "appropriate" or "not appropriate," and even that you're "too old" to do certain things. (Wrong!)

Exercise 3:

1. What are five personal qualities you feel that you want to change in your life?

2. What are five <u>new</u> personal qualities you want to incorporate into your new life?

3. Write at least two paragraphs on what you need to do in order to accomplish this.

4. After doing all of these exercises, take some time to discuss them with a close friend or family member (who can listen to what you have to say and not judge you or give you their opinions unless you ask for them). By doing this you will begin to free up your restricted beliefs about what is possible in your life and you will begin to do the things in your life that bring you joy.

Escaping the cycle of conflict is a journey. It will take you to places you never knew you could go. If you adhere to the concepts in this book and keep your attention on your children and your future in a positive light, your life will begin to settle down and you will find that the joy in your life returns.

Your unrestricted life starts as soon as you allow it, why wait? Do the things that bring you joy, live your dreams and teach your children to live theirs.

The chains that bind you to conflict are those of your own beliefs and nothing more. Other people don't control your behavior and actions—only you can do that. The change you are looking for in every aspect of your life is within your grasp if only you are willing to have the vision and the courage to watch it unfold.

I hope this book serves you well. Keep it near. When you feel lost in the process, pick it up again.

---

[i] The High Conflict Diversion Program™. Brook Olsen 2009
[ii] Amato, Paul R, and Booth, Alan A. *A Generation at Risk; Growing Up in an Era of Family Upheaval.* Cambridge, Massachusetts: Harvard University Press, 1997. (page 220)
[iii] (reference removed)
[iv] Janet R. Johnston "Future of Family's"

References

Amato, P.R. (2005). The impact of family formation change on the cognitive, social, and emotional well -being of the next generation. *Future of Children, 15,* 75-96.

Booth A. and Amato, P.R. (2001). Parental pre divorce relations and offspring post divorce well-being. *Journal of Marriage and Family, 63,* 197-212.

Brodie, K. (2001). [Review of the book *The co-parenting survival guide: letting go of conflict after a difficult divorce*]. *Library Journal, 126,* 13.

Donner, M.B. (2006). Tearing the child apart: the contribution of narcissism, envy, and perverse modes of thought to child custody wars. *Psychoanalytic Psychology, 23,* 542-553.

Eddy, B. (2004). *Splitting. Protecting yourself while divorcing a borderline or narcissist.* Roswell, GA: Eggshells Press.

Eddy, B. (2006). *How personality disorders drive family court litigation.* Retrieved from: http://www.eddylaw.com/articles/vol2_no1_art4.htm

Friedman, M. (2004). The so-called high-conflict couple: a closer look. *The American Journal of Family Therapy, 32,* 101-117.

Gilmour, G. (2004). *High conflict separation and divorce: Options for consideration.* Paper presented to Family, Children and Youth Section, Department of Justice, Canada. Retrieved from: http://www.justice.gc.ca/eng/pi/pad-rpad/rep-rap/2004_1/2004_1.pdf

Gow, K.M. (1999). Letting go: for physical, emotional, and spiritual health. *Journal of Religion and Health, 38,* 155-166.

Johnston, J. R. (1994). High-conflict divorce. *The Future of Children, 4,* 165-182.

Johnston, J.R. (2006). A child-centered approach to high-conflict and domestic-violence families: differential assessment and interventions. *Journal of Family Studies, 12,* 15-35.

Johnston, J.R. and Roseby, V. (1997). *In the name of the child.* New York: The Free Press.

Kelly, J. B. (1993). Current research on children's post-divorce adjustment: no simple answers. *Family Court Review, 31,* 29-49.

Kelly, R.F., Redenbach, L. and Rinaman, W. (2005). Determinants of sole and joint physical custody arrangements in a national sample of divorces. *American Journal of Family Law*, *19*.

Lebow, J. (2003). Integrative family therapy for disputes involving child custody and visitation. *Journal of Family Psychology*, *17*, 181-192.

Lowenstein, L. (2000). Play therapy with children in crisis. *Journal of Interpersonal Violence, 15.*

Macooby, E.E. and Mnookin, R.H. (1992). *Dividing the child.* Cambridge, MA: Harvard University Press.

Margolin, G. (2001). Co-parenting: a link between marital conflict and parenting in two-parent families. *Journal of Family Psychology, 15,* 3-21.

Nichols, K.S. (2006). Breaking impasses. Strategies for working with high conflict personalities. *American Journal of Family Law.*

Portnoy, S.M. (2004). The role of judges in keeping difficult parties contained in court. *American Journal of Family Law, 18,* 133-134.

Richardson, S. and McCabe, M.P. (2001). Parental divorce during adolescence and adjustment in early adulthood. *Adolescence*, *36*, 467-489.

Schramm, D. G. (2002, August). *The costs of divorce in Utah.* Presentation of findings from a study on the economic consequences of divorce in Utah to Utah's Governor's Commission on Marriage, Salt Lake City, UT.

Stahl, P. M. (2008). *Parenting after divorce.* Atascadero, CA: Impact Publishers.

Wallerstein, J., Lewis, J. and Blakeslee, S. (2000). *The unexpected legacy of divorce: a 25 year land mark study.* New York: Hyperion.

Thank you to Susannah H. Michalson for her help in compiling and editing the References

Made in the USA
Middletown, DE
04 March 2020